NAUGHTY SHAKESPEARE

MICHAEL MACRONE

ILLUSTRATIONS BY TOM LULEVITCH

CADER BOOKS • NEW YORK

Andrews and McMeel
A Universal Press Syndicate Company
Kansas City

Thank you for buying this Cader Book—we hope you enjoy it.
And thanks as well to the store that sold you this, and the hardworking sales rep who sold it to them. It takes a lot of people to make a book. Here are some of those people who were instrumental:

EDITORIAL: Jake Morrissey, Dorothy O'Brien, Polly Blair, Nora Donaghy
DESIGN: Charles Kreloff
COPY EDITING/PROOFING: Bill Bryan
PRODUCTION: Carol Coe, Traci Bertz, Cathy Kirkland
LEGAL: Renee Schwartz, Esq.

Printed in United States of America

If you would like to share any thoughts about this book, or are interested in other books by us, please write to:
Cader Books, 38 E. 29 Street, New York, NY 10016

Or visit our web site: http://www.caderbooks.com

Library of Congress Cataloging-in-Publication Data

Macrone, Michael.
    Naughty Shakespeare! / Michael Macrone : illustrations by
Tom Lulevitch. — 1st ed.
      p. cm.
    Includes bibliographical references (p.   ) and index.
    ISBN 0-8362-2757-3 (hd.)
    1. Shakespeare, William, 1564-1616—Quotations.   2. Shakespeare,
William, 1564-1616—Criticism and interpretation.   3. Bawdy poetry—
England—History and criticism.   4. Social problems in literature.
5. Vulgarity in literature.   6. Swearing in literature.   7. Racism in literature
8. Sex in literature.   9. Quotations, English.
I. Title.
PR2892.M34   1997
822.3'3—dc21   97-2728
                                                                                 CIP

June 1997

First Edition

10 9 8 7 6 5 4 3 2 1

Contents

Preface

Naughty? Shakespeare? That's probably not what your teacher told you. But the most sublime poet in English was also the most all-encompassing; and the Bard encompassed a lot of things people wish he hadn't.

That includes a fair helping of sex, violence, crime, horror, politics, religion, anti-authoritarianism, anti-Semitism, racism, xenophobia, sexism, jealousy, profanity, satire, and controversy of all kinds. As you might guess, Shakespeare pushed a lot of buttons in his day—which is one reason he was so phenomenally popular. Despite what they tell you, people *like* having their buttons pushed. And to this day, the Bard keeps pushing them, although they're not all the same buttons.

Shakespeare's work isn't just a "little" naughty. Naughtiness is part of its very texture. Even if we just limit ourselves to dirty jokes—laying violence, politics, and the rest aside—there aren't many plays or poems you could call "clean." *Julius Caesar* and *Macbeth* come close, and if you ignore Bottom and the other tradesmen (which isn't easy), so does *A Midsummer Night's Dream.* Not coincidentally, these are three of the four plays most often taught in American high schools. The fourth is *Romeo and Juliet,* but God knows what teachers do with *that.* (Practically everything Mercutio utters is dirty, and that's just the beginning.)

The seamier side of Shakespeare has long been hidden not only from children, but also from adults. The movement to "sophisticate" the Bard began shortly after his death and reached full speed by the end of the 17th century. Shakespeare appeared on stage only in more "decorous" adaptations, mend-ing his incorrect plots and striking "low" scenes of bawdy talk and bad behavior. Critics of taste judged that whole scenes and even plays were inauthentic, or improvised by actors, for Shakespeare was too good to have written them.

For the next two centuries, Shakespeare's genius was increasingly idolized, even as offensive material was cut, ignored, or explained away. Some people even forgot it was ever there. Meanwhile, the frank language of an earlier and "cruder" time fell into disuse, and its political controversies faded from memory. By the 20th century, explaining such things had become the business of tedious and distracting footnotes. Thus we have protected ourselves from offense, and enhanced the silly notion that the Bard was some sort of prophet of virtue.

Naughty Shakespeare briefly attempts to correct the situation. I can do no more than sample from the nearly endless supply of disturbing material in Shakespeare's plays and poems—and, partly to keep the size manageable, I focus almost exclusively on the plays. Some outstandingly gross and truly horrible lines, alas, have escaped comment here. But I hope there's enough to convince you that when the Bard was bad, he was *really* bad.

Those who prefer to keep their image of Shakespeare as Pure Poet and Upholder of Tradition are advised to return this book to the shelf. For I cannot promise, as does Lucio in *Measure for Measure,* that "If bawdy talk offend you, we'll have very little of it." On the contrary, we're going to have lots of it. Buttons will be resolutely pushed. And I hope you agree with me that outrage only makes the Bard better—for pure poetry and upholding tradition are ultimately pretty boring.

Texts and Abbreviations

I quote Shakespeare's texts, with occasional slight alterations, from the single-volume *Riverside Shakespeare*. (For publication details, see "References," page 209.)

Many authorized and pirated editions of Shakespeare's works were published in his lifetime and shortly thereafter. We cannot be sure how complete and correct any of these editions might be, though we can guess which ones most closely approximate Shakespeare's manuscripts. Even the legendary "First Folio" is unreliable, though it was edited and authorized by his colleagues. It contains numerous editorial and typographic errors, and it lacks lines and scenes present in earlier "quartos"—cheap single-play editions, roughly analogous to today's paperbacks. ("Folio" and "quarto" refer to page size; folio pages are twice as large as quarto pages.)

Nonetheless, editors do rely heavily on the First Folio, which was a good effort to present a clean and complete collection of Shakespeare's works. For one thing, it contains all the plays now agreed to have been written by Shakespeare alone, though it does lack *Pericles* (which is mostly if not all Shakespeare's) and *The Two Noble Kinsmen* (of which he wrote a substantial portion). (On the other hand, it includes *Titus Andronicus* and *Henry VIII,* which some critics doubt are solely the Bard's.) The Folio is our only authoritative source for eighteen plays; as for the rest, modern editors choose the best text from among the Folio and earlier quartos, carefully collating editions and restoring readings they believe represent Shakespeare's intentions.

However, not all editors agree on what the "best" text is in every case, or on exactly how corrupt (and why) the others are. The *Riverside* edition presents a fairly rational, consistent, and conservative version of the texts, which—along with its ready availability in America—is why I use it here. I also make occasional use of readings from The Arden Shakespeare, a paperback series with excellent notes and supplementary materials. Both *Riverside* and the Arden volumes mark the significant divergences among the various early editions.

■ ■ ■

When quoting from plays, I locate phrases and speeches by act, scene, and line number(s), separated by periods. Thus "IV.ii.134–36" refers to act 4, scene 2, lines 134 through 136.

In quoting from Shakespeare's sonnets, I use two Arabic numerals: the first for the sonnet, and the second for the line number. Thus "*Sonnets,* 23.12" refers to line 12 of the 23rd sonnet. For other poems, I cite only the line number.

Often when referring to plays and poems, I abbreviate the titles; here is a key, along with *Riverside*'s guesses on dates of composition:

1 Henry VI	*The First Part of Henry the Sixth* (1589–90; revised 1594–95)
2 Henry VI	*The Second Part of Henry the Sixth* (1590–91)
3 Henry VI	*The Third Part of Henry the Sixth* (1590–91)
Richard III	*The Tragedy of Richard the Third* (1592–93)
Venus	*Venus and Adonis* [poem] (1592–93)
Errors	*The Comedy of Errors* (1592–94)
Sonnets	*Sonnets* [poems] (1593–99?; published 1609)
Complaint	*A Lover's Complaint* [poem] (1593?; published 1609)
Lucrece	*The Rape of Lucrece* [poem] (1593–94)

Titus	*The Tragedy of Titus Andronicus* (1593–94)
Shrew	*The Taming of the Shrew* (1593–94)
TGV	*The Two Gentlemen of Verona* (1594)
LLL	*Love's Labor's Lost* (1594–95; revised 1597)
John	*The Life and Death of King John* (1594–96)
Richard II	*The Tragedy of King Richard the Second* (1595)
Romeo	*The Tragedy of Romeo and Juliet* (1595–96)
MND	*A Midsummer Night's Dream* (1595–96)
Merchant	*The Merchant of Venice* (1596–97)
1 Henry IV	*The First Part of Henry the Fourth* (1596–97)
Wives	*The Merry Wives of Windsor* (1597; revised ca. 1600)
2 Henry IV	*The Second Part of Henry the Fourth* (1598)
Much Ado	*Much Ado about Nothing* (1598–99)
Pilgrim	*The Passionate Pilgrim* [poems by various hands] (?; published 1599)
Henry V	*The Life of Henry the Fifth* (1599)
Caesar	*The Tragedy of Julius Caesar* (1599)
AYL	*As You Like It* (1599)
Hamlet	*The Tragedy of Hamlet, Prince of Denmark* (1600–1)
Phoenix	*The Phoenix and the Turtle* [poem] (ca. 1601)
TwN	*Twelfth Night, or What You Will* (1601–2)
Troilus	*The History of Troilus and Cressida* (1601–2)
AWW	*All's Well That Ends Well* (1602–3)
Measure	*Measure for Measure* (1604)
Othello	*The Tragedy of Othello, the Moor of Venice* (1604)
Lear	*The Tragedy of King Lear* (1605)
Macbeth	*The Tragedy of Macbeth* (1606)
Antony	*The Tragedy of Antony and Cleopatra* (1606–7)
Coriolanus	*The Tragedy of Coriolanus* (1607–8)
Timon	*The Life of Timon of Athens* (1607–8)
Pericles	*Pericles, Prince of Tyre* (1607–8)
Cymbeline	*Cymbeline* (1609–10)
WT	*The Winter's Tale* (1610–11)

Tempest	*The Tempest* (1611)
Henry VIII	*The Famous History of the Life of Henry the Eighth* (1612–13)

Some scholars believe that *Pericles* and *Henry VIII* were collaborations, the former with an unknown author and the latter with John Fletcher. (Fletcher succeeded Shakespeare as his company's regular playwright.) The once-popular view that Shakespeare did not write all of *Titus Andronicus* has been steadily losing ground. In the end, this is all speculation. The only surviving play that was published then, and is accepted now, as a collaboration (with Fletcher) is *The Two Noble Kinsmen* (1613), which I leave aside in this study.

OTHER ABBREVIATIONS

References such as "(Gurr, 134)" refer to specific pages in the works listed on page 209—in this case, page 134 of Andrew Gurr's *Playgoing in Shakespeare's London*. Additionally, I use the following abbreviations:

Arden	The Arden Shakespeare
Folio	*Mr. William Shakespeares Comedies, Histories, & Tragedies* [1623]—the "First Folio"
OED	*The Oxford English Dictionary*
Riverside	*The Riverside Shakespeare*

Will's Naughty Theater

William Shakespeare (1564–1616) lived in a naughty time and worked in a naughty business. As he began his career in London, sometime in the late 1580s, civic leaders and religious authorities considered the theater extremely disreputable and even dangerous. In 1594, the Lord Mayor of London pleaded with Queen Elizabeth's Privy Council to tear down all the theaters, for they were

> places of meeting for all vagrant persons and masterless men
> that hang about the City, thieves, horse-stealers, whore-
> mongers, cozeners [cheaters], cony-catching persons [con
> men], practicers of treason, and other such like. (Gurr, 134)

Because London's city fathers were so vehemently opposed to the business, theatrical impresarios had to locate their playhouses beyond the reach of the aldermen. So they set up shop in seedy nearby suburbs ("liberties"), side by side with alehouses, bordellos, and bear-baiting arenas.

The mayor had a point. The crowds at Elizabethan amphitheaters included a conspicuous number of idlers, ruffians, thieves, and prostitutes; the plays they watched (including Shakespeare's) were often violent, provocative, and bawdy. As far as London's authorities were concerned, playhouses were dens of potential crime, riot, and treason. In the eyes of many others, the whole experience was harmful to public morals.

Joining city leaders in the crusade against playhouses were Puritans and other conservative moralists. Their problem with the theaters went beyond public behavior to the larger problem of the moral influence. Plays had been defined for centuries—for a millennium—as a form of instruction; they please, but they also teach. By depicting virtue rewarded and vice punished, plays provide not only moral precepts but also patterns for better behavior. The Puritan critic Phillip Stubbes turns this argument on its head, and shakes it violently, in his antitheatrical tract *The Anatomie of Abuses* (1583):

> You say there are good Examples to be learned in [plays]. Truly, so there are: if you will learn falsehood; if you will learn cozenage; if you will learn to deceive; if you will learn to play the hypocrite, to cog, lie, and falsify; if you will learn to jest, laugh, and fleer, to grin, to nod, and mow; if you will learn to play the vice, to swear, tear, and blaspheme both Heaven and Earth; if you will learn to become a bawd, unclean, and to devirginate maids, to deflower honest wives; if you will learn to murder, flay, kill, pick, steal, rob, and row; if you will learn to rebel against princes, to commit treasons, to consume treasures, to practice idleness, to sing and talk of bawdy love and venery; if you will learn to deride, scoff, mock, & flout, to flatter & smooth; if you will learn to play the whoremaster, the glutton, drunkard, or incestuous person; if you will learn to become proud, haughty, & arrogant; and, finally, if you will learn to contemn God and all his laws, to care neither for heaven nor hell, and to commit all kind of sin and mischief, you need to go to no other school, for all these good examples may you see painted before your eyes in interludes and plays.

Modernized and slightly polished, this tirade would nicely suit our own self-appointed moral guardians as they rail against the evils of Hollywood.

■ ■ ■

You may be wondering at this point why the government didn't simply shut the theaters down and save everyone a lot of trouble. The answer is that the Crown, that is, the monarch and her courtiers, found the public theaters useful. The drama's inherent persuasive power—its ability to make fiction look real—could serve the government's interests as much as anyone's. Numerous Elizabethan plays celebrated pious and patriotic values; the Crown may have regarded the favor as cheaply purchased, if the price was only a little titillation.

Besides, courtly audiences enjoyed titillation too. Many of the same plays Shakespeare's company staged for the public were also performed at court, where professional acting companies provided the main entertainment. If the queen or any of her cohorts ever objected to what they saw, we don't know about it. Not that playwrights could get away with anything; as we shall soon see, certain material was deemed off-limits. But as for broader complaints about the immorality of plays and the dangers of playgoing, the government largely brushed them off.

Stubbes was obviously a crank, but that's not the only reason the Court ignored him. The monarch required not just entertainment, but high-quality entertainment—that is, plays that had been tested and refined in performance, and players who were limber and well-rehearsed. Both Queen Elizabeth I (reigned 1558–1603) and her successor King James I (reigned 1603–25) were connoisseurs of the drama, and they would hardly have deprived themselves of crack performers by allowing the theaters to be closed. And while acting companies were paid handsomely for their courtly appearances, they had largely to support themselves.

So playing to the public both kept them in practice and kept them in business.

On the other hand, while neither as paranoid as the mayor nor as puritanical as Stubbes, the Crown did agree that both players and playhouses had to be controlled. In times of plague or a serious political crisis, the government did close down the theaters, occasionally for extended periods. (Shakespeare wrote most of his poetry while the playhouses were shuttered in 1593.) Only in James's reign were adult players allowed back into London (where boys' companies had performed for a few years), and even then they were confined to smaller and more exclusive "private" halls. This compromise with city authorities lasted until 1642, when antitheatrical Puritan parliamentarians, having overthrown King Charles I, shut down all the theaters for twenty years.

Actors and other public performers were also subjected to official control. In the eyes of the law, they were little better than what the mayor called "vagrant persons and masterless men." This meant that to practice their trade they first had to find a "master," that is, a sponsor with a peerage. Shakespeare's company, for example, was sponsored in the years 1596–1603 by George Carey, Baron Hunsdon, who became Elizabeth's lord chamberlain. Thus they were known as "the Lord Chamberlain His Servants" or, more briefly, "the Lord Chamberlain's Men." (After 1603, King James adopted the company as his own, and they thus became "the King's Men.")

By tying the company's survival to the good graces of a powerful government official, the Crown more or less kept the players in line. But just to make sure, it required that all plays first be approved, and if necessary censored, by the Master of Revels, who booked entertainment at court and oversaw public spectacles. What was not acceptable for public consumption tended to vary with the political climate and the particular

Master of Revels; but "sedition and heresy" would be a rough definition.

While *censorship* is a dirty word in the U.S., the British government has often found it a useful and flexible tool. The British public seems to live with it, having no special taste for things such as libel and incendiary speech. Preventing religious or political violence may take precedence over free discourse— whether it be the discourse of a playwright or the discourse of a guerrilla. The crowds at Shakespeare's theaters were reportedly given to emotional moods, and one can understand that the government might want to prevent their getting too emotional about extremely hot subjects.

One shouldn't confuse the idea of what is "dangerous" with the idea of what is "offensive." Elizabethans took personal *insults* very seriously, but they had a very different notion of personal *offense*. (It appears to have been a rather small notion, given the paltry evidence for it.) As we'll see in "Lost Scenes from Shakespeare's Histories" (page 51), the Master of Revels expunged a number of the Bard's politically sensitive scenes. But he apparently had no complaints about Shakespeare's "dirty" language ("talk of bawdy love and venery," as Stubbes put it). This may strike the reader as curious, and we shall return to the puzzle shortly.

One special case of "offensive" language was eventually barred, both from the stage and from print. Prior to 1606, published works were policed by the ecclesiastical courts, whose mandate paralleled that of the Master of Revels—they were mostly looking for sedition and heresy. The religious authorities weren't even as efficient and consistent as the Revels Office, but presumably printed matter required less scrutiny. It's one thing to stage the deeds (and misdeeds) of kings before a gaping illiterate crowd, and another thing entirely to present them for the sophisticated reflection of a literate elite.

In any case, the year 1606 brought a new act that consolidated these disparate censorial duties under the Revels Office. Titled the Act to Restrain Abuses of Players, it also augmented the list of prohibited subjects with "jestingly or profanely" invoking "the holy Name of God or of Christ Jesus, or of the Holy Ghost or of the Trinity." All by itself, this act radically reduced the verbal impact of a few of Shakespeare's characters—such as Sir John Falstaff and Ancient Pistol—who were wretchedly profane in texts before 1606, and only terribly profane thereafter. (See "'God's Lid' and Other Offensive Oaths," page 79.)

Not that there was tons of material in Shakespeare's work blatant enough to censor. The Bard was a professional, and he was no dummy; he certainly had a fairly good idea of what would fly and what wouldn't. On the other hand, he sometimes pushed the limits, partly perhaps to test their extent, but mostly for the sake of maximum excitement. The thrills of conflict and controversy kept the crowds returning for more.

Shakespeare usually sidestepped the censor, but he managed to keep his plays emotionally provocative. His philosophical musings and soaring speeches are regularly punctuated by violence, slapstick, personal abuse, passionate outbursts, bawdy episodes, and other material we now find more "offensive" than anything the censor cut.

■ ■ ■

Shakespeare's England, in the midst of a cultural renaissance and newly embarked on New World conquests, was full of energy, ambition, and newfound wealth. But it was also unsettled, violent, skeptical, and often paranoid. For better or for worse, it was a very dramatic age, a time when all the world seemed a stage.

This also meant that one was always in a sense "on display." Shakespeare's contemporaries were much less solitary, less interior, and (dare I say) less repressed than we are today. Scholars debate whether an Elizabethan would have understood what we mean by "privacy" (or even by "self"), but nobody doubts that it was a more fulsome, explicit, and demonstrative age.

Later commentators would deplore Elizabethans as "rude" and "unsophisticated," which meant that they had different standards of social and verbal propriety. But while it took more to offend them, Shakespeare's contemporaries were not entirely lacking in decency. Certain sorts of behavior and language were seen even then as low-class or puerile, and most of the powerful four-letter words had been tabooed for centuries.

Elizabethan propriety had mostly to do with class: It was a code of what certain sorts of people should and shouldn't do or say. What people were willing to hear is another matter entirely. Verbal extravagance, violence, bile, and bawdy were hallmarks of literature high and low. Passion, corruption, disease, and death were handled boldly and frankly. Scenes of anguish, terror, and lust were played to audiences of both sexes and all classes.

Even children were brought to the theaters, and many of the tradesmen's apprentices who flocked there were in their early teens. Though their bourgeois husbands were known to discourage them, city wives still ventured to the suburbs. This was a time when women and children were spared the sort of coddling they'd receive thereafter. By the 18th century, English society had evolved more "modern" notions of decency, and gentlemen better understood what was fit for ladies and children (especially daughters) to know.

The profanities excised from Shakespeare's texts were initially just those involving the deity—"God's bread," "'Zounds," and the like (page 79). By the turn of the 18th century, other defects had become more glaring, and they would be omitted from Shakespearean adaptations and later from the Bard's original texts, as they were revived. Critics and dramaturgs generally agreed that Shakespeare was much more presentable without the regrettable "barbarities" of language and action to which, as a rude Elizabethan, he was prone.

Take the sorry case of *Othello,* the most popular tragedy of the 17th century, and Shakespeare's most passionate play. It comes to pass, in the original text, that the hero is so over-whelmed by sexual jealousy that he begins to act very badly. In one horrifying scene (IV.i), Iago and Othello begin by debat-ing the precise circumstances of Desdemona's alleged infideli-ties—"naked with her friend in bed," "Lie with her? lie on her?"—in terms thought too explicit for family consumption. By the mid-18th century, such lines would be absent from all acting texts of *Othello.* Another 174 lines were also cut from the scene, beginning where the overwrought Moor has an epileptic seizure and falls into a trance; this and later details were found to spoil the "tragic" effect.

Elsewhere, indecent language—which pervades the play—was softened or cut. Iago's news to Brabantio that "an old black ram/ Is tupping your white ewe" was deleted (I.i.88–89), as, needless to say, were more shocking lines such as "Would you, the supervisor [spectator], grossly gape on?/ Behold her topp'd?" (III.iii.395–96) and "Cassio did top her" (V.ii.136). The word *cuckold* vanished. Othello no longer called his wife an "Impudent strumpet" or a "whore" (IV.ii.81, 86); Desdemona no longer punned, "I cannot say 'whore.'/ It does abhor me now I speak the word" (161–62). The word abhorred so many that it virtually disappeared from plays and print by the 19th century.

These neutered stage versions of *Othello* also became best-selling booklets, outselling editions of the uncut works. (Un-cut, but still tampered with; Alexander Pope, for instance, had already changed those two *top*'s to milder *tup*'s.) Particularly popular was the expurgated collection assembled in 1773–74 by the aptly named Francis Gentleman, who had already offered many helpful suggestions in *The Dramatic Censor* (1770). On Othello's invocation of "devils" and his demand that they "roast me in sulphur" (V.ii.277–79), Gentleman characteristically wrote, "as [these lines] convey very horrid ideas, we could wish them omitted." Often, they were.

Such efforts to save the Bard from himself culminated in the famous *Family Edition* of Shakespeare (1818), edited by Thomas Bowdler and an unnamed close relative, probably his sister. In the words of Marvin Rosenberg, Bowdler's compelling motive was "to protect the purity of British womanhood from indecent language.... Shakespeare's words were simply too potent to be trusted with a lady" (244–45). Bowdler himself wrote that the Bard's plays are "stained with words and expressions of so indecent a nature that no parent would chuse to submit them in uncorrected form to the eye or ear of a daughter."

Some examples of Bowdler's improvements, still from *Othello:* Iago no longer tells Brabantio that "your daughter and the Moor are now making the beast with two backs" (I.i.115–17), but rather that "your daughter and the Moor are now together." In Shakespeare, the bloodthirsty hero worries that Desdemona's "body and beauty" will distract him from his purpose (IV.i.205); in Bowdler, her body is deleted. "Top" is gone, and "tup" along with it, and "naked" for good measure. Shakespeare's "bawdy wind that kisses all it meets" (IV.ii.78) is reduced to a "very wind."

Bowdler's efforts, which in truth weren't nearly so extreme as Gentleman's, earned him gratitude in his century and infamy in ours. The *Family Edition* is now out of print, and *bowdlerize* is a term of contempt. Yet Shakespeare has never really recovered; many of those who read the complete texts and understand them are even today embarrassed by his low comedy and incorrect ideas.

▪ ▪ ▪

In any case, between about 1750 and about 1950, it was either censored Shakespeare or no Shakespeare; so we must partly thank Gentleman and Bowdler for keeping his plays alive and onstage. Thus Shakespeare has reigned virtually uninterrupted since at least 1594, the year of his first published work, a quarto of *Titus Andronicus*. (This wildly popular play would ironically become Shakespeare's most reviled effort—see "Bloody Shakespeare," page 24.)

But Shakespeare's greatness in the eyes of history has latterly become a burden. It's scarcely possible any more to simply experience his plays as pure literature—or pure entertainment—for the word "pure" has become impure. Like the terms "great" and "literature," it is inevitably tainted by some agenda.

On one side are those who question whether "great" means anything more than "approved by self-appointed (and oppressive) cultural authorities." On another side are those who use "great" to mean "spiritually and morally superior"— that is, "better" for us than mere "entertainment." There are, as you might imagine, numerous variations on these themes. All have been applied at one point or another to Shakespeare, the most prominent of literary targets.

There's no remaining neutral in the "culture wars"; and, given a title like *Naughty Shakespeare,* you might assume I think the moralists are wrong. To a degree, I do; to urge Shakespeare on students and the populace at large as a great upholder of traditional values (as the moralists understand "traditional"), you have to explain away a good deal of gratuitous dirt and violence. And, worse, you have to crudely simplify Shakespeare's complex, if not confused, moral attitudes—of which there are many.

But while I do think a simplistic moral view is absurd, I also believe that the bad stuff—of which there's enough to offend anybody—only increases the work's power, even its moral power. The debunkers and relativists are wrong, too, if they think Shakespeare is "great" only because cultural elites have decreed it so. And by aiming to replace the canon of dead white males with an "improved" version that's more positive and uplifting, they are no less moralistic in their way than the moralists.

Thanks to their efforts—and thanks also to student diversity and demands for more freedom—it is now possible to major in English at any of a number of respected American colleges without studying Shakespeare. Given the Bard's heretofore unmatched stature and influence, this is a remarkable turn of events. And given his vast influence on later English and American literature, it's also unwise. It's all well and good to treat students as free consumers of learning, but in a literal sense they're not yet *educated* consumers.

From one angle, the situation is deplorable; but it does have its positive side. Arguments like "Shakespeare's no longer relevant," or "Reading Shakespeare is a form of oppression," are obviously ludicrous; but on the other hand, Shakespeare has perhaps been hurt more than helped by decades of academic sanctimony.

■ ■ ■

After all, though he's the king of English letters, Shakespeare *was* a mere mortal. It was far from obvious in his day that his work would prove of lasting value, and for at least a century Ben Jonson and John Fletcher were esteemed his equals. His subsequent idolization—a.k.a. "Bardolatry"—has distorted Shakespeare's true place in literary history; and it has set his work on a false pedestal, encouraging reverence more than understanding.

Believe it or not, not everything he wrote is perfect, or timeless, or even good, by whatever measure you choose. But since the 18th century, Shakespeare has served as a totem of literature's power to perfect reality and in turn to perfect its readers. Reading his work or attending performances is supposed to make you better—more aware, more knowing, and in some sense more virtuous. He's become Western culture personified, the embodiment of Tradition and thus a key link to the "eternal values" that always seem to be slipping away.

The very idea would have made his contemporaries

laugh—and Shakespeare would have laughed with them. As far as he was concerned, he was an entertainer, committed to the twin goals of enchanting his audience and making pots of money. And in the eyes of many Elizabethans, his chosen medium, the theater, was as far from "uplifting" as you could get. Rather than temples of moral improvement, the theaters were viewed as "bawdy houses" (brothels) where one went to be corrupted.

Elizabethan critics such as Stubbes made the same mistake as all would-be censors: to assume that entertainments are capable of corrupting morals on contact. This is the same mistake, in reverse, as assuming that morally "good" literature implants good values directly in our souls.

Latter-day moralists, ignoring the attitudes of Shakespeare's own contemporaries, have tended to place him squarely on the side of the angels. But if he were really all that healthful, he'd probably have been forgotten long ago; at best, he'd be ranked with such pious figures as Bunyan. Shakespeare's greatness depends in large part on two factors inconvenient to literary utilitarians: He was a great entertainer, not above feeding his audience what it wanted; and his work is morally extremely complex.

The Bard's reputation is so intimidating that people sometimes forget he was an entertainer, not the author of cultural prescriptions, nor a promoter of the traditional values of his day. In this book I aim not to present a "true" picture of Shakespeare's mind—virtually impossible in any case—but a *truer* picture of his work than what is usually taught, and of what has usually, through the centuries, been performed.

In his *Book of Virtues,* William Bennett cites six uplifting passages from the Bard. And he's correct to do so, for the Bard gives voice to many noble ideals and to much timeless wisdom. But I'm delighted to outweigh him in my little book of vices. Keep *Naughty Shakespeare* by your copy of Bennett's *Virtues;* read them both; or, better yet, read the plays.

Bloody Shakespeare

Today's moral crusaders routinely condemn Hollywood for foisting sex and violence on society, as if Hollywood had invented sex and violence. These people clearly haven't seen many of Shakespeare's plays, some of which give the most violent and shocking movies a run for their money. I'm not just talking about small stuff like carving up a dictator on-stage in *Julius Caesar*, or removing Gloucester's eyes—"Out, vile jelly!"—in *King Lear*. I'm talking about plots that are practically soaked through with blood.

Thanks to Bardolatry and Shakespeare's institution as "our greatest poet," people tend to forget that he wrote for the popular stage. We may read him in our studies and classrooms, savoring the exquisite poetry and high-minded philosophy, but there wasn't much percentage for the Bard in philosophy. While most of his playwriting peers were mere poets-for-hire, Shakespeare was a shareholder (as well as dramatist and actor) in his company. And from what we know of his life, he took making money pretty seriously. This meant drawing crowds: big crowds, and not just the literate, wit-loving courtiers and law students. This meant staging astounding—and sometimes extremely violent—dramas for the masses.

Throughout his career, but especially in the 1590s, Shakespeare's audience showed a marked taste for brash and aggressive spectacles, such as patriotic military tales full of swordplay and noise. (It was a decade of ongoing conflict with the hated Spanish.) Another sort of play that pleased the public palate was the "revenge tragedy," typically full of horror, cruelty, blood, fear, and evil in general. By far the most popular spectacle of its day was Thomas Kyd's horrific revenge play *The Spanish Tragedy* (ca. 1588), which, along with his now-lost early version of *Hamlet,* must have deeply impressed the young Shakespeare.

Kyd's (and Shakespeare's) bewitching, idea-crammed poetry may have been the main draw for some; but it also gave an intellectual veneer to less lofty gratifications. One might despise crude horror, but crude horror with an idea becomes art. Many playgoers then, like many moviegoers today, actually *wanted* to be shocked, frightened, or even disgusted. You might call such emotions degrading or prurient; but Aristotle had a more ennobling word for them: catharsis.

And catharsis was a proven moneymaker. In the Elizabethan phase of his career (roughly 1590 through 1603), far more successful than any of Shakespeare's comedies were his two revenge tragedies, *Titus Andronicus* and *Hamlet.* His bloody and tragic first history cycle, comprising *Henry VI, Parts 1–3* and *Richard III,* was also a major early hit and proof of the Bard's box-office potential. The violent and otherwise unwholesome *Othello* would go on to prove his most successful tragedy ever.

Perhaps you're still not convinced that Shakespeare can stand up to most of the movies the moralists get exercised over. All we need to do is take a more detailed look at his first (and most gruesome) tragedy, which you won't soon see performed by a high-school drama club.

The Tragedy of Titus Andronicus

*Note: In addition to disgusting crimes and shocking violence, Titus is full of wicked puns and foul language. Examples of these are set in **boldface** type. (See also "Shakespeare's Lewd Lexicon," page 181.)*

THE BACKGROUND: The noble general Titus Andronicus has led Rome to victory against the barbaric Goths. He returns to Rome with the Gothic queen Tamora in tow, along with her sons and her lover, Aaron the Moor. Titus refuses the people's offer of the Roman crown, backing the elder of the former emperor's two sons, Saturninus.

ACT I

Titus's sons perform a human sacrifice, offering up Tamora's son Alarbus to appease some restless ghosts. "Alarbus' limbs are lopp'd,/ And entrails feed the sacrificing fire" (I.i.143–44). Titus then offers his daughter Lavinia in marriage to Saturninus, but Saturninus's brother Bassianus, who's already proposed, abducts her. When one of Titus's sons stands in the way of pursuit, Titus kills him. Saturninus, insulted by the whole business, marries the bewitching Tamora instead.

Recap: 1 human sacrifice, 1 murder

ACT II

Tamora may be Rome's new empress, but Aaron is determined to continue to "**mount aloft**" and "wanton" with her (II.i.13, 21). Tamora's sons, meanwhile, grow hot at the thought of mounting Lavinia. Aaron thinks that "some certain **snatch** or so" would cool them down, and he helps them plot the rape. Get her in a dark forest, he advises; "There speak, and strike, brave boys, and take your turns;/ There serve your lust, shadowed from heaven's eye,/ And revel in Lavinia's **treasury**" (II.i.129–31). The unsuspecting Lavinia, now in the forest with Bassianus on a hunt, comes across Tamora and ironically praises her "goodly gift in **horning**"—that is, in screwing around with Aaron, whose blackness Bassianus insults (II.iii.67, 72). Soon enough, Tamora's sons stab Bassianus and exult in the prospect of raping Lavinia on top of his corpse. But this is too much even for them, so they throw the body in a ditch and drag Lavinia offstage. There they take their pleasure, and for good measure they cut out Lavinia's tongue and cut off her hands, so she won't be able to finger them.

Recap: 1 murder, 2 rapes, 3 amputations

ACT III

Aaron contrives to frame two of Titus's three remaining sons for the murder of Bassianus. He tells Titus that if an Andronicus cuts off his hand and sends it to Saturninus, his sons will be spared. Titus himself insists on lending a hand, and Aaron helps remove it. But Aaron lied, and in return Titus gets his sons' heads, plus his own hand, which wasn't needed. Lavinia gets to carry the hand around in her mouth. Titus concludes that Lavinia is probably best off killing herself, which she can do by removing the hand and using her mouth to hold a knife.

Recap: 2 executions, 1 amputation

ACT IV

Still alive, Lavinia eventually realizes that even without hands, she can still write: she takes a staff in her mouth and traces the names of her rapists in the dirt. Titus isn't surprised—fitting sons to a mother who "lulls" Saturninus while "she **playeth on**

her back" (IV.i.99). Proof is forthcoming when Tamora gives birth to a black-skinned baby boy—who the nursemaid remarks is "as loathsome as a toad/ Amongst the fair-fac'd breeders of our clime" (IV.ii.67–68). When one of Tamora's sons upbraids the Moor for "undoing" his mother, Aaron replies, "Villain, I have **done** your mother" (76). Then he murders the nurse. Elsewhere, Titus, having lost more of his mind, contrives to have an innocent clown hanged by Saturninus. Meanwhile Titus's last living son, Lucius, joins with the Goths and marches with an army on Rome.

Recap: 1 murder, 1 execution, 1 birth out of wedlock, 1 act of treason

ACT V

Just outside Rome, Lucius runs into Aaron, who's fleeing the city with his bastard son. After insulting Aaron's race for a while, Lucius orders both father and baby hanged. To spare his child, Aaron spills all the beans about the evil doings of Tamora, her sons, and especially himself, exulting in his own depravity, atheism, and general badness. Lucius decides hanging's too good for him.

Back in Rome, everybody views Titus as a harmless lunatic who might be used to stop Lucius from attacking. But Titus has other ideas. The first is to cleverly trap Tamora's two sons and murder them. The second is to chop them up and make meat pies for dinner. At a banquet he serves these tasty morsels to Tamora, who "daintily" feeds, while Titus prepares more entertainments. First he kills Lavinia to put her out of her misery. Then he reveals the whereabouts of Tamora's sons, to which she says nothing because Titus stabs her first. Saturninus responds by killing Titus, then Lucius responds by killing Saturninus. (The mighty Bard manages to pack these last three murders into four lines.) Being the only one left standing, Lucius takes over Rome. His first act as emperor is to order that Aaron be buried up to his neck and left to starve, and that Tamora's corpse be thrown out for beasts and carrion birds to feed on. The End.

Recap: 6 murders, 1 execution

GRAND TOTAL

1 human sacrifice, 9 murders, 4 executions, 2 rapes, 4 amputations, 1 act of treason, and 1 birth out of wedlock. The Hollywood execs are green with envy.

■ ■ ■

Titus is so over the top that some people refuse to believe Shakespeare wrote it, or at least that he wrote all of it. Editors in the 18th and 19th centuries printed it, but only under duress. Edward Ravenscroft, who adapted the play in 1687, spoke for many when he said that *Titus* was "the most incorrect and indigested piece in all [Shakespeare's] Works; It seems rather a heap of Rubbish than a Structure."

People like this underestimate the Bard and neglect the fact that *Titus* is very much in the style of its time. But let's humor them for a moment and turn to a better-written play that nobody doubts is entirely Shakespeare's—though you may still have trouble digesting it.

The Tragedy of Richard the Third

THE BACKGROUND: As the play begins, the sons of York—Edward, Clarence, and Richard—have wrested the throne from Henry VI. They achieved this by stabbing the crown prince to death, while Richard took care of Henry himself—his second murder before the play even starts. So now Edward IV sits in the throne while Richard, deformed from birth, broods.

ACT I

Apparently, Richard won't be happy till he's king, and he's going to do whatever it takes to get there. First he arouses his brother King Edward against his other brother Clarence, and then, fearing Edward's resolve, orders Clarence murdered. Next he barges in on Henry VI's funeral procession to seduce the dead king's wife. Conveniently, Edward, an adulterer, falls ill, just as an assassin stabs Clarence in the Tower of London and deposits his body in a cask of wine.

Recap: Merely 1 assassination, but a particularly nasty one.

ACT II

When Edward hears of Clarence's death he feels incredibly guilty and then dies. Has Richard, with his two elder brothers out of the way, realized his dream to be king? Not yet. There's the bothersome business of the ex-king's son, Prince Edward, who's on his way to London to be crowned. There are also the Queen's allies, who make their hatred of Richard no secret. Richard throws them all into a tower and hides the key.

Recap: 1 death of natural causes. Is Shakespeare slipping?

ACT III

Richard contrives to have Prince Edward and his beloved little brother lodged in the Tower of London. Cloaking his designs, Richard tests the loyalty of his friends. One who fails is Lord Hastings, whom Richard orders executed on the pretext that Hastings is having an affair with Edward IV's old mistress, an alleged witch. Richard also executes the Queen's allies, which is another three. The populace is starting to get restless at this point, so Richard and his pal Buckingham stage a huge show of Richard's great virtue and total indifference to power. The crowd at least pretends to buy the act, so they offer Richard the crown he pretends not to want.

Recap: 4 executions, and back on track.

ACT IV

In his hour of triumph, Richard's thoughts turn to more killing. He decides his charismatic nephews are simply too irritating to live, a notion even his closest friend Buckingham finds a bit much. As resistance forms at home and in France, where the son of Henry VI stews in exile, Richard goes on a spree. He gets rid of his wife, perhaps with poison, and begins cleaning house of other potential threats. He hires a shady type named Tyrrel to have his nephews the princes smothered in the Tower. Buckingham, knowing he's next, joins forces with Richmond, Henry VI's son, but then he's captured.

Recap: 1 murder, 2 assassinations

ACT V

Buckingham is executed. Richard marches to meet Richmond at Bosworth Field. But the night before his big day the ghosts of all his victims appear to curse him and bless Richmond. To make a long story short, Richard loses his horse, and then Richmond kills him. It was a pretty brief reign, but fun while it lasted.

Recap: 1 execution; thousands dead on the battlefield, including Richard.

GRAND TOTAL

3 assassinations, 9 executions, 1 murder, 1 death from natural causes, and thousands dead on the battlefield. That more than makes up for the play's lack of sex.

▪ ▪ ▪

Since we might be accused of focusing too much on Shakespeare's earlier work, which we know is less virtuous than his later, how about if we take a quick look at the greatest of them all, the play that stands at the very center of Western Literature.

The Tragedy of Hamlet, Prince of Denmark

THE BACKGROUND: Old King Hamlet of Denmark is murdered by his brother Claudius, who then marries the widowed queen.

SYNOPSIS

Act I: The ghost of the old king tells Hamlet what happened. Hamlet vows revenge. His lover Ophelia grows distant, on the advice of her busybody father, Polonius, the new king's counselor.

Act II: Hamlet acts insane and thinks some more on revenge. Claudius gets two of Hamlet's friends, Rosencrantz and Guildenstern, to spy on him.

Act III: Hamlet puts on a play at court which shows Claudius that the prince is wise. Hamlet thinks some more on revenge. While yelling at his mother, Hamlet kills Polonius behind a curtain. Claudius decides to pack Hamlet off to England, with secret orders that he be executed.

Act IV: Things don't go as Claudius planned. Hamlet escapes, leaving Rosencrantz and Guildenstern to the fate meant for him. Ophelia goes mad and sings naughty songs before drowning herself. Her brother, Laertes, vows revenge, and teams up with Claudius to plot Hamlet's death.

Act V: Hamlet and Laertes have a fencing match. Laertes mortally wounds Hamlet. Hamlet kills Laertes. The queen drinks poison, and then Hamlet kills Claudius.

GRAND TOTAL

4 murders, 2 executions, 1 suicide, 1 death by poison. Augmented by a fair helping of bawdy banter, plus state corruption and rampant hypocrisy.

■ ■ ■

Admittedly, the gore is more plentiful in Shakespeare's earliest plays. But there's more than sufficient killing to get the blood moving in "masterpieces" such as *Caesar, Romeo, Othello,* and *Macbeth.* And let's not forget the power of verbal abuse and threatened violence, which could also bring down the house. Readers are directed to Henry V's explicit and bloodcurdling threat to murder, rape, spoil, and pillage the town of Harfleur in *Henry V* (III.iii.1–41).

"O Happy Dagger": Promoting Suicide

S uicide has never ranked high on the Christian morality scale. Even in our own morally bankrupt times, many still consider it a very grievous sin. All the more so in Shakespeare's England. An important (unanswered) question in *Hamlet* is whether Ophelia meant to drown herself; because if she did then she's an outcast from God. "Is she to be buried in Christian burial," wonders her gravedigger, when she "willfully seeks" her own damnation? (*Hamlet,* V.i.1–2). Any kind of murder, self-murder included, is a mortal sin. What makes suicide even worse is despair, acted out in a final severance from God's forgiveness. To die with a mortal sin on your soul, in the doctrine of *Hamlet,* is to go straight to hell. Suicide is the devil's choice.

Given all that, it's a little strange that so many of Shakespeare's good guys wind up killing themselves. Far from a disgrace or moral outrage, suicide is often a noble gesture, or at least an appropriate end. It can even be powerfully alluring: Romeo and Juliet would be much less beautiful, Othello less grand, Brutus less heroic, if they survived their plays. Shakespeare's attitude seems more Roman than English, more pagan than Christian. Either way, you won't find the following suicide scenes (complete with last words) in William Bennett's next uplifting tome.

1. ROMEO

Here's to my love! [*Drinks.*] O true apothecary!
Thy drugs are quick. Thus with a kiss I die. [*Dies.*]

Romeo and Juliet, V.iii.119–20

2. JULIET

Yea, noise? Then I'll be brief. O happy dagger, [*Taking
        Romeo's dagger.*]
This is thy sheath [*stabs herself*]; there rust, and let me
        die. [*Falls on Romeo's body and dies.*]

Romeo, V.iii.169–70

3. PORTIA (WIFE OF BRUTUS)

Kills herself offstage when things start looking bleak for Brutus. "With this she fell distract," he reports, "And (her atten-
dants absent) swallow'd fire" (*Julius Caesar*, IV.iii.155–56).

4. CASSIUS

Guide thou the sword. [*Pindarus stabs him.*] Caesar, thou
        art reveng'd,
Even with the sword that kill'd thee. [*Dies.*]

Caesar, V.iii.45–46

5. BRUTUS

Farewell, good Strato. [*Runs on his sword.*] Caesar now be
        still,
I kill'd not thee with half so good a will. [*Dies.*]

Caesar, V.v.50–51

6. OPHELIA

Drowns offstage in a "weeping brook" (*Hamlet*, IV.vii.175). Whether it was legally suicide is controversial.

7. OTHELLO

And say besides, that in Aleppo once,
Where a malignant and a turban'd Turk
Beat a Venetian and traduc'd the state,
I took by th' throat the circumcised dog,
And smote him—thus. [*He stabs himself.*]...
I kiss'd thee ere I kill'd thee. No way but this,
Killing myself, to die upon a kiss.

[*Falls on the bed and dies.*]

Othello, V.ii.352–59

8. LADY MACBETH

At the end of *Macbeth*, Malcolm speaks of Lady Macbeth as the "fiend-like queen,/ Who (as 'tis thought) by self and violent hands/ Took off her life" (*Macbeth*, V.ix.35–37). We're to assume he's right, but Shakespeare was nodding to the fuzzy historical record.

9. EROS

My dear master,
My captain, and my emperor: let me say,
Before I strike this bloody stroke, farewell....
Why, there then. [*Kills himself.*] Thus I do escape the sorrow
Of Antony's death.

Antony and Cleopatra, IV.xiv.89–95

10. MARC ANTONY

Come then; and, Eros,
Thy master dies thy scholar: to do thus
                    [*Falling on his sword.*]
I learnt of thee. How, not dead? not dead?
The guard, ho! O, dispatch me!
                    [*Finally dies 98 lines later.*]

Antony, IV.xiv.101–4

11. CLEOPATRA

Come, thou mortal wretch,
          [*To an asp, which she applies to her breast.*]
With thy sharp teeth this knot intrinsicate
Of life at once untie. Poor venomous fool,
Be angry, and dispatch....
As sweet as balm, as soft as air, as gentle—
O Antony!—Nay, I will take thee too;
                    [*Applying another asp to her arm.*]
What should I stay— [*Dies.*]

Antony, V.ii.303–12

12. CHARMIAN

[*Applies an asp.*] O, come apace, dispatch! I partly feel
          thee....
Ah, soldier! [*Charmian dies.*]

Antony, V.ii.321–28

13. IRAS

Her death is not explicitly described, but it precedes Cleopatra's and Charmian's in their triple suicide. Cleopatra admires the gentleness of Iras's death and concludes, in an apostrophe to the corpse, that "This proves me base" (*Antony,* V.ii.300)—that is, ignoble not to have killed herself first.

Out of this baker's dozen, only two suicides are *not* romanticized—Ophelia's and Lady Macbeth's. Perhaps not coincidentally, both happen offstage and both are somewhat doubtful. All the men and the rest of the women kill themselves in grand heroic strokes. A senseless loss of life, to be sure; but it's all for the good of the plays, which wouldn't have climaxes otherwise. Once you're drawn into the plot, only a suicide (or four) will get you out. Thus Shakespeare glorifies the act.

As for a strong defense of life and of sticking it out, we do have the line, "Why should I play the Roman fool, and die/ On mine own sword?" It's delivered by the butcher Macbeth, at the beginning of the scene in which he meets his well-deserved end (*Macbeth,* V.viii.1–2).

Down with the Establishment!

After sorting through the wreckage of Shakespeare's tragedies and histories, critics have still discovered redeeming themes. All the murderous kings, appalling violence, and senseless suffering in Shakespeare's plots aren't, they say, just pitiful and horrifying; they also convey an idea. In one popular version, the idea is that Shakespeare loved authority and hated disorder—which must be why he depicts so much rebellion and disorder (you know, to show what happens when authority is mocked). "Shakespeare's most important political point," according to enthusiast Charles Boyce, is "that all social good derives from a stable monarchy" (85).

Without the help of such critics, you might develop different impressions. The principal effect of Shakespeare's tragedies and histories strikes the naive viewer as somehow less uplifting. And themes do not readily jump out from such plays as the three parts of *Henry VI*. In fact, the murderous rebel Jack Cade steals the show in part 2, as Shakespeare's efforts to make him evil are defeated by his instincts to make him funny. For a supposed authoritarian, the Bard seems oddly fond of characters like Hotspur, who leads an uprising against the unlikable Henry IV. And what are we to do with the degenerate Sir John Falstaff, riot incarnate, who is simultaneously Shakespeare's most popular creation and a very poor spokesman for order and authority?

Whether Shakespeare's weak kings and attractive rebels exist despite his political sympathies or because of his theatrical sense, they make it more difficult to sell a canned political moral. If Shakespeare was bad at anything, it was canned morality. Nor did he excel at producing conventional accounts of "great men," which traditionally focused on the famous (or infamous) deeds of beings who resembled walking allegories more than living persons.

Kings and queens, Caesars and tyrants, were portrayed as exceptional figures driven by grandiose notions, extraordinary passions, and divine will—not all of which necessarily harmonized. They are set apart from the common run of humanity, to whom their motives are ontologically if not rationally inaccessible. These great figures address readers and audiences in an artificial, highly stylized, elevated rhetoric, very grand but also very off-putting.

Such is also the case with the casts of Shakespeare's earlier history plays. The cardboard characters spout labored rhetoric and generally take the roles of puppets on historical string. Even the devilish Richard III, with all his self-revealing soliloquies, is essentially a stage figure and not a believable character to whom we could "relate."

Yet Shakespeare's early plays are still more human than any others from the period; his later plays, more so. From *King John* on, he brings his rulers down much closer to the ground. They are not simply agents of God (or the gods, or Fate), but also men and women with common human feelings and failings. As Samuel Johnson said, Shakespeare's "story requires Romans or kings, but he thinks only on men" (28). Even though most monarchs still spout grandiose set-pieces, they also betray more intimate and familiar concerns.

Such humanizing adds psychological texture to the plays, but at the expense of awe. Brutus muses on the fate of Rome, but he also argues with his wife at home. Caesar may "bestride the narrow world/ Like a Colossus" (*Caesar,* I.ii.135–36), but we also know he's a poor swimmer, an epileptic, and a conceited fool. Macbeth is both the tool of inscrutable supernatural powers and a man susceptible to common doubts and fears.

While Shakespeare's technique makes such characters more credible and more poignant, it also subverts the familiar and sharp distinctions between kings and commoners. Henry may look almost perfect in *Henry V,* but his past as Prince Hal in the *Henry IV* plays would embarrass even the House Ethics Committee. Others had written of the failings of Richard II, Henry VI, and Richard III, but no one had ever portrayed them so clearly as mere human beings with ordinary failings, magnified (sometimes to monstrosity) by circumstance.

In short, Shakespeare to a greater or lesser degree "domesticates" his monarchs and dukes. This wasn't just a radical literary move, but also, at least latently, a radical political move. Shakespeare's monarchs may have thought themselves divinely anointed and thus elevated above mere mortals, but the poet presents them to us as all too human, and all too vulnerable.

So far as we know, no one in the government complained about Shakespeare's dramatic techniques, except when he came too close to current affairs. His skeptical attitude toward the royal mystique is confined largely to the past or to legends, which was safe. But such skepticism had a hidden momentum, and when it gained full force it would lead, thirty-three years after Shakespeare's death, to the deposition and later the execution of King Charles I.

On the whole, the Bard displays a marked lack of awe for authority and for the establishment in general. Rare is the ruler or patriarch who is as wise or as good as he pretends to be. Even Henry V, whose myth Shakespeare was loath to deflate, leaves us feeling uneasy, as if we'd been tricked. As for the rest, they are generally corrupt, incompetent, foolish, or otherwise deeply flawed. The people in charge have some serious problems. What follows is a brief report.

Rotten Rulers and Other Problematic Authority Figures

Historical Kings of England

KING JOHN

REIGNED: 1199–1216
APPEARS IN: *King John*

Humiliates both himself and England in dealing with the French and later with the Pope; orders the assassination of his own nephew, who has a more legitimate claim to the throne; dies after being poisoned by a monk. In his last words he aptly sums himself up as "but a clod/ And module [hollow image] of confounded royalty" (*John*, V.vii.57–58).

KING RICHARD II

REIGNED: 1377–99
APPEARS IN: *Richard II*

A corrupt weakling; has his uncle murdered; bungles a domestic brouhaha and thus sets the stage for the War of the Roses; first abdicates to Henry Bolingbroke (Henry IV) and then, after facing a kangaroo court, lets himself be deposed; delivers self-pitying verses until he's assassinated at Henry's suggestion; for more, see "Lost Scenes from Shakespeare's Histories" (page 51).

KING HENRY IV

REIGNED: 1399–1413
APPEARS IN: *Richard II, 1 Henry IV, 2 Henry IV*

Dubbed a "vile politician" by his charismatic opposite, Hotspur; his idea of political leadership is to "busy giddy minds/ With foreign quarrels" (*2 Henry IV,* IV.v.213–14) and to distract the populace with a (never realized) crusade against the Infidel; comes to power by "indirect crook'd ways" (184), namely by dethroning the legitimate king and having him killed, which leads to a troubled reign of perpetual insurrection; and then he complains about how rough life is as king.

KING HENRY V

REIGNED: 1413–22
APPEARS IN: *1 Henry IV, 2 Henry IV, Henry V*

Easily the most virtuous ruler in all the history plays. Of course, in his youth he did fraternize with thieves and prostitutes; and he's not above packing off his old crony Falstaff to Fleet Prison. And as for his heroic war in France, it's instigated by sophistical clergymen to distract the country from proposed church reforms. At the walls of Harfleur, Henry promises rape, infanticide, "murther, spoil, and villainy" (*Henry V,* III.iii.32) if the town resists (they don't); and in a later moment of panic he orders the slaughter of helpless French prisoners. The Romantic critic William Hazlitt called Henry "a very amiable monster"; the modern critic Herschel Baker calls his wooing of the French princess "ursine." Is this the best Shake-speare can do?

KING HENRY VI

REIGNED: 1422–61, 1470–71
APPEARS IN: *1 Henry VI, 2 Henry VI, 3 Henry VI*

A pious figurehead at best. Though he's the nominal monarch in three history plays, he's his own personal leadership vacuum. First the tool of corrupt advisers and then the tool of his wife, he sits out the deciding battle of his reign and mopes on a hill. Dethroned by the Yorkists and then restored by the Lancastrians, he resigns the crown he's too weak to wear. Killed by Richard III in the Tower of London.

KING EDWARD IV

REIGNED: 1461–70, 1471–83
APPEARS IN: *2 Henry VI, 3 Henry VI, Richard III*

An adulterer. In *Henry VI, Part 3* he helps his brothers stab to death Prince Edward, Henry's heir.

KING RICHARD III

REIGNED: 1483–85
APPEARS IN: *2 Henry VI, 3 Henry VI, Richard III*

Quite simply, a butcher. Richard is responsible for 11 deaths by murder, assassination, and execution, leaving aside his exploits on the battlefield. Mostly he hands the dirty work off to proxies, such as the assassin he hires to kill his own brother Clarence. In the end, conscience makes a coward of him and he's slain in battle with the future Henry VII.

KING HENRY VIII

REIGNED: 1509–47
APPEARS IN: *Henry VIII*

Shakespeare treads lightly on the grounds of more recent English history—so lightly that Henry barely appears in his play. (It's more *The Tragedy of Cardinal Wolsey* than *Henry VIII*.) When Henry does show up he listens to bad advice, executes a loyal peer, cheats on his wife, and then divorces her. Which all turns out great, since England gets rid of the Pope, and Henry's second wife brings forth Elizabeth, later a very famous queen.

■ ■ ■

Other Historical Figures

KING MACBETH OF SCOTLAND

REIGNED: 1040–57
APPEARS IN: *Macbeth*

Bewitched by the prophecies of three "weird sisters," Macbeth murders King Duncan. Then he murders his friend Banquo. Then he has Macduff's wife and children murdered. Everyone hates him, and, even worse, he hates himself too.

LADY MACBETH, QUEEN OF SCOTLAND

APPEARS IN: *Macbeth*

Cajoles Macbeth until Duncan is dead, at which point she begins to lose her mind, and then she kills herself.

JULIUS CAESAR, ROMAN DICTATOR

REIGNED: 49–44 B.C.
APPEARS IN: *Julius Caesar*

More than the historical Caesar, Shakespeare's seems to envy a crown, which, if the Bard was such a monarchist, should be good news. But in fact he turns out both weaker and more arrogant. Shakespeare adds fear of water and physical debilities to his character; has him speak in the royal "we" while not yet a king; and makes him smug and self-satisfied. "Danger knows full well," he pronounces, "That Caesar is more dangerous than he./ We are two lions litter'd in one day,/ And I the elder and more terrible" (*Caesar,* II.ii.44–47). Moments before his death, he proclaims himself no ordinary man (III.i.37) and informs Casca that "I spurn thee like a cur out of my way" (46). One speech later, he observes that he is to mankind as the North Star is to the heavens; among all men, "I do know but one/ That unassailable holds on his rank,/ Un-shak'd of motion; and that I am he" (68–70). Such hubris basically means that the guy was asking for it.

CAESAR AUGUSTUS, ROMAN TRIUMVIR AND EMPEROR

REIGNED: 43–29 B.C. (as triumvir); 27 B.C.–A.D. 14 (as emperor)
APPEARS IN: *Julius Caesar, Antony and Cleopatra*

At least as worthy the title "vile politician" as Henry IV, Augustus (called Octavius in *Caesar*) is efficient but also cold and calculating, at times Machiavellian. In his roles he is the very embodiment of order, bringing two tragedies to a close by thwarting his enemies and firmly grasping the reins of state. In both cases, we're rooting for his enemies (Brutus and Cassius in *Caesar*, Antony and Cleopatra in *Antony*).

■ ■ ■

This is a fairly grim accounting, but it must be admitted that the Bard had the historical record to contend with. He may have enhanced a character here and there, but if they are wicked on stage it is only because they were wicked in life. (Or at least wicked in the chronicles Shakespeare pillaged for his plays.) So it must have been a relief to the author when he turned to fiction; for in fiction he was free to idealize his kings and queens and dukes in the image of his own desires.

It's true: Shakespeare's fictitious rulers are not generally corrupt and murderous, allowing for the exception of Claudius in *Hamlet*. However, they also generally appear in comedies, where corruption and murder are off the point. On the whole these authorities are harmless, though they are also mostly fools. Even the tragic or tragicomic rulers make asses of themselves: Lear divides his kingdom between two evil daughters while disowning the good one; Leontes disgraces his throne and all but kills his wife and children in a fit of irrational jealousy; Cymbeline of Britain is an ineffectual monarch manipulated by his vile wife.

The rest are of the ilk of King Ferdinand of Navarre, who haplessly presides over *Love's Labor's Lost*. Absurdly plotting to make his court a "little academe" (I.i.13), he swears his courtiers to a life of pure contemplation, free from worldly temptations, including the opposite sex. But he immediately crumples upon the arrival of some lovely French ladies. Kings like Ferdinand don't actually appear to do very much, and when they do they manage to nicely screw things up. Take Duke Vincentio in *Measure for Measure*, who's botched his job so badly that he has to go into hiding while someone else finally enforces the law. Then, disguised as a priest, he spies on his subjects and administers bogus sacraments.

The list of dubious dukes and kings is a long one. Equally numerous are feckless patriarchs (monarchs of their families), whose principal business is to stand in the way of their children's happiness. They are meddlesome killjoys whose patriarchal rule must be overthrown, and, especially in comedy, they are regularly defied, ridiculed, and abused. (Rigid old men with lusty offspring were stock figures in classical and Renaissance drama.)

In *The Two Gentlemen of Verona*, for example, the Duke of Milan does precious little ruling, but spends most of his time scheming to marry his daughter to an old (rich) fool. Egeus in *A Midsummer Night's Dream* is even more contrary; though his daughter Hermia loves Lysander, he tells her she's going to marry Demetrius or else take her pick between life in a nunnery or death. Shylock is such a fun father that *his* daughter steals his ducats and runs away from home. Then there are the fathers Montague and Capulet...but we'll leave the story here, to be resumed later in "Family Values Watch" (page 130).

Lost Scenes from Shakespeare's Histories

The Tudors learned at least one lesson from the bloody civil wars of the 15th century: If they wanted to stay on the throne, they had better put down the bishops and the lords. Henry VIII (reigned 1509–47) set the tone when he declared himself supreme head of both church and state, reliant on no one but God for his authority. The boundaries of dissent were constricted while those of sedition were generously expanded. Henry kept his throne while around him heads rolled—some of them belonging to former wives.

His daughter Elizabeth (reigned 1558–1603) was, to the relief of all, somewhat less capriciously brutal; but one was still well advised to avoid open criticism. This went double for playwrights and actors, who if they couldn't police themselves would find the Crown doing it for them. Any mention of Elizabeth herself obviously had to be fawning at worst, and treatments of history had to avoid anything remotely threatening to the state.

Shakespeare's histories were no exception, and their sometimes fulsome chauvinism verges in places on state propaganda. But the patriotic speeches can obscure the larger picture, which is much more problematic. And unless you're willing to wade through scholarly notes, you may never know that certain passages were considered dangerous enough for the royal censor to suppress.

The Bard's enormously popular plays on the War of the Roses—*Henry VI, Parts 1–3* and *Richard III*—illustrate some of the problems. On the plus side, propaganda-wise, they demonstrate that God has his eye on affairs of state, and that at some higher level (not always apparent at the time) he rewards the good and punishes the bad. The monster Richard III, for example, is brought down with no little help from Heaven. The problem, though, is that *all* the kings are bad. Not only is Richard III a butcher, but Henry VI is a weakling and Edward IV is corrupt (see pages 30–31). This doesn't add up to a ringing endorsement of the Tudor notion that all monarchs are God's chosen—unless God is just choosing to punish one with the next.

■ ■ ■

But these plays were popular not for their political commentary—which is often incoherent anyway—but because they're stuffed full of horrible crimes, astonishing violence, anti-French jingoism, plots, schemes, and bellicose rhetoric. In short, they're deliberate crowd-pleasers, and if that renders the political moral unclear, so be it.

In any case, the violence and moral ambiguity in themselves didn't seem to bother the Crown. In fact, as far Elizabeth was concerned, the worse some of her predecessors looked, the better. What concerned the government were more explicit allusions and actions that might be taken to reflect directly on the queen. And the queen's Master of Revels (overseer and censor of plays—see page 15) found some disturbing things indeed in several of Shakespeare's histories.

The Bard probably had little desire to get himself and his successful company in trouble. If he had any unorthodox political or religious ideas, he kept them well hidden. His main ambition seems to have been to keep his theater full; and this required making the plays as provocative and dramatic as possible without running afoul of the Revels Office.

The chronicle histories he drew on already dealt with royal corruption, civil conflict, insurrections, regicide, and other controversial topics. How controversial depended both on the current political climate and the method of presentation. The chronicles couched history in patriotic, pro-Tudor themes, so that past disasters are redeemed by present glory. It was another matter, however, to act these disasters on stage, without the benefit of a narrator and for the consumption of excitable crowds.

Some of Shakespeare's presentations were apparently deemed too exciting. For example, a somewhat corrupted but still revealing early quarto of *2 Henry VI* contains the following passage:

> [*Alarms, and they fight, and York kills Clifford.*]
>
> *York.* Now, Lancaster, sit sure, thy sinews shrink;
> Come, fearful Henry, grovelling on thy face,
> Yield up thy crown unto the Prince of York.
>
> [*Exit York*]

The mockery of King Henry ("Lancaster"), the invitation to "grovel," and the demand that he yield up his crown are all missing from the later, "official" version of the play in Shakespeare's First Folio. Somebody must not have liked them, and that somebody could well have been the Master of Revels. In place of York's speech in the early text, the Folio reads,

> *York.* Thus war hath given thee [Clifford] peace, for thou art still.
> Peace with his soul, heaven, if it be thy will!
>
> [*Exit*]
>
> *2 Henry VI,* V.ii.29–30

—an altogether more pious, and less dangerous sentiment. The Folio also modifies another of York's seditious speeches from the previous scene:

> *York.* Base fearful Henry that thus dishonor'st me,
>   By heaven, thou shalt not govern over me;
>   I cannot brook that traitor's presence here,
>   Nor will I subject be to such a King,
>   That knows not how to govern nor to rule.
>   Resign thy crown, proud Lancaster, to me,
>   That thou usurped has so long by force,
>   For now is York resolv'd to claim his own,
>   And rise aloft into fair England's throne.

The Folio version (V.i.91–105) is just as scornful and biting, but the phrase "Base fearful Henry" is nowhere to be found, nor is "Resign thy crown," nor is York's explicit vow to "rise aloft into fair England's throne." We can't be sure Shakespeare wrote exactly what appears in the quarto, but it's probably a close approximation.

▓ ▓ ▓

The same history also features that altogether objectionable rebel leader, Jack Cade, whose very presence may be one reason the quarto, published in 1594 and again in 1600, was not reprinted between 1600 and 1619. (From 1600 to her death in 1603, Elizabeth felt herself in some danger, as did her successor, James, in the early years of his reign.) Cade is a low-class rabble-rouser who, at the instigation of York, presents himself as "Lord Mortimer" and attempts to stir up a popular movement to depose Henry and crown himself king. In the quarto he's heralded this way:

Nick. But sirrah, who comes more beside Jack Cade?

George. Why there's Dick the butcher, and Robin the saddler, and Will that came a-wooing to our Nan last Sunday, and Harry and Tom, and Gregory that should have your Parnill, and a great sort more is come from Rochester, and from Maidstone, and Canterbury, and all the towns hereabouts; and we must all be lords or squires, as soon as Jack Cade is king.

This detailed and impressive accounting of hearty countrymen perhaps made Cade—the would-be usurper—seem too popular with ordinary folk, for it's replaced with a much briefer and more mocking passage in the Folio:

Holland. I see them, I see them! There's Best's son, the tanner of Wingham—

Bevis. He shall have the skins of our enemies, to make dog's-leather of.

Holland. And Dick the butcher—

Bevis. Then is sin struck down like an ox, and iniquity's throat cut like a calf.

Holland. And Smith the weaver—

Bevis. Argo [i.e., Ergo], their thread of life is spun.

Holland. Come, come, let's fall in with them.

2 Henry VI, IV.ii.21–30

This cuts Cade down to size, and his followers down to buffoon-ish proles, but other passages were equally explosive. Some time after 1600, a scene in which Cade knights Dick the Butcher was suppressed—probably under James I (reigned 1603–25), who was widely resented for knighting just about anyone who could pay for the privilege. (Though James went further, Elizabeth also knighted many an "unworthy" man—

Sir Andrew Aguecheek in *Twelfth Night* is an Elizabethan specimen.)

In the quarto, Stafford, the king's deputy, demands that the "base drudge" Cade yield himself "unto the King's mercy," to which Cade rejoins, "Nay, bid the King come to me, and [if] he will, and then I'll pardon him; or otherwise I'll have his crown, tell him, ere it be long." This, like York's similarly impudent speeches, is predictably cut from the Folio, as is Cade's vow in the next scene (IV.iii) to "sit in the King's seat at Westminster" on the morrow.

Cade's threats against the king weren't the only elements of his scenes that might, in the authorities' view, incite an audience of tinkers and saddlers to riot. There's Dick's famous line—the most famous in the play—"The first thing we do, let's kill all the lawyers" (IV.ii.76–77). Maybe the Master of Revels sympathized with the utopian sentiment, for the line stayed in; also spared is a passage in which Cade orders a clerk to be hanged on the grounds that he can actually write his own name. But the following lines were just too much:

[*Enter Dick and a sergeant.*]

Sergeant. Justice, justice, I pray you sir, let me have justice of this fellow here.

Cade. Why, what has he done?

Sergeant. Alas sir, he has ravished my wife.

Dick. Why, my lord, he would have 'rested me, and I went and entered my action in his wife's paper house. [Obviously some obscure bawdy joke.]

Cade. Dick, follow thy suit in her common place. [*To sergeant:*] You whoreson villain, you are a sergeant, you'll take any man by the throat for twelve pence, and 'rest a man when he's at dinner, and have him to prison ere the meat be out of his mouth. Go, Dick, take him hence, cut out his tongue for cogging [ly-

ing], hough [hamstring] him for running, and, to
conclude, brain him with his own mace. [*Exit Dick
with sergeant.*]

The wonder is not that such invitations to torture officers of
the law and to rape their wives were cut, but that the censors
left so much alone in the Folio, which almost certainly repre-
sents a version acted on the Jacobean stage. Cade *is* shown to
be a brutal anarchist, and his rebellion *does* fail, but *any* depiction of rebellion could be considered dangerous, especially at
times when the queen or king felt vulnerable.

▪ ▪ ▪

The point of Elizabeth's maximum vulnerability came shortly
after the turn of the century, thanks partly to Robert Dev-
ereux, Earl of Essex. Essex was one of his age's most exalted
men. After a successful military action in Spain in 1596, he became a popular hero and moved into the queen's inner circle.
But Essex was also temperamental, vain, and undisciplined.
When in a heated exchange the queen struck him, he very un-
wisely drew his sword—the first bad move in what would
prove to be his steady decline.

After things had cooled down, Elizabeth sent Essex to Ireland in March 1599 to put down an anti-imperial revolt. Six
months later, Essex was back in England, unbidden, having
miserably failed in his task—in fact, having only concluded a
humiliating and unauthorized pact with the rebels. A furious
Elizabeth put Essex on trial in 1600; as a result, the proud earl
was stripped of his title—the ultimate Elizabethan dishonor.

In the hopeful months before this disgrace, Shakespeare
included one of his few allusions to current events in the manuscript of *Henry V* (1599). After comparing the triumphant
Henry to Caesar, Shakespeare anticipates the king's return
from conquered France to the welcome of delirious crowds:

> As by a lower but loving likelihood,
> Were now the general of our gracious Empress,
> As in good time he may, from Ireland coming,
> Bringing rebellion broached on his sword,
> How many would the peaceful city quit,
> To welcome him!

Henry V, V.Chorus.29–34

Though qualified ("lower...likelihood," "As in good time he may"), this is still gross flattery. We don't know what drove Shakespeare to include it; perhaps it was genuine admiration for Essex, perhaps a wish to please his former patron the Earl of Southampton, a devotee of Essex. (Shakespeare had dedicated his poems *Venus and Adonis* and *The Rape of Lucrece* to Southampton, who is also the likeliest candidate for the "Young Man" of the *Sonnets.*)

Whatever his motive, Shakespeare surely came to regret it. If the Chorus's lines were ever presented on stage, they were certainly excised in the summer of 1599, as Essex's failure became obvious; at any event, like all the play's choruses, they're absent from early quarto texts, though present in the Folio.

The most alarming lines in the passage are "How many would the peaceful city quit/ To welcome him"—which is exactly what Essex would soon hope for (see below). Any large gathering was viewed by authorities as a potential riot in the making (which is one reason they feared the theater), let alone a large popular gathering behind an ambitious nobleman who had drawn his sword on the queen.

Matters came to a head in the early months of 1601. On February 8, Essex launched an abortive coup, first unsuccessfully marching on the court and then unsuccessfully attempting to rally London behind him. The afternoon before, hoping to prime the populace, one co-conspirator, Sir Geley Meyrick, had hired Shakespeare's company (for a pretty penny) to exhume and publicly perform their old history, *Richard II*.

This tragic text presents the sad tale of a poetic but ineffectual king deposed and then murdered by command of the usurper Henry Bolingbroke, later King Henry IV (and presumably a model for Essex). According to Francis Bacon, famous essayist and the rebels' prosecutor, Meyrick had hoped that "his lord should bring [the tragedy] from the stage to the state, but that God turned it upon their own heads" (Schoenbaum, 218–19).

Meyrick certainly got less than his money's worth. Not only did London give Essex the cold shoulder, Meyrick was quickly hanged, joined later by Essex on February 24. As for Shakespeare and his men, they thankfully managed to escape the noose (as did Southampton, who was in on the plot; he got off with a long stay in the Tower of London). In fact, the queen was so forgiving that they found themselves performing for her at court on February 23—the eve of Essex's execution. One assumes they didn't play *Richard II*.

▨   ▨   ▨

On the other hand, Elizabeth didn't soon forget the episode. In August 1601 she remarked, "I am Richard II. Know ye not that?" She went on to complain, somewhat cryptically, that "this tragedy was played forty times in open streets and houses" before the attempted coup. To what performances she refers we haven't much of a clue, but we do know that *Richard II* had already run into trouble after its first run on the boards, most likely in 1596. So much seems clear from the Elizabethan editions, published in 1597–98, for they all lack a key scene present in later texts and the Folio.

Toward the middle of the play, Richard, sneering at Bolingbroke's threat, voices a version of the Tudor theory of monarchy:

> Not all the water in the rough rude sea
> Can wash the balm off from an anointed king;
> The breath of worldly men cannot depose
> The deputy elected by the Lord;
> For every man that Bolingbroke hath press'd
> To lift shrewd steel against our golden crown,
> God for his Richard hath in heavenly pay
> A glorious angel; then if angels fight,
> Weak men must fall, for heaven still guards the right.
>
> *Richard II,* III.ii.54–62

In act IV, however, his angels desert him.

Weakened by his own greedy actions, his love of flattery, and a failed Irish expedition, the unpopular Richard is captured by the aggrieved and ambitious Bolingbroke, who leads the King to London as a prisoner. Disaffected nobles at Elizabeth's court would also be complaining about high taxes, pernicious flatterers, and a failed Irish policy (which would ironically only get worse thanks to Essex).

In the early texts of act IV, scene i, Bolingbroke brings his enemies to Parliament to be tried for treason; the loyal Bishop of Carlisle delivers a stirring but futile defense of Richard; the King, offstage, abdicates the throne; and then Bolingbroke announces the date of his coronation. But in the uncensored version, something worse happens between Richard's abdication and Bolingbroke's announcement. In an extra 165 lines, Richard is hauled in person before Parliament, where he's forced to admit to "grievous crimes" so that "the souls of men/ May deem that you are worthily depos'd" (IV.i.223–27). After Richard retails dozens of lines of self-pitying verse, Bolingbroke actively deposes him and orders him sent to the Tower.

This so-called deposition scene became one of Shakespeare's most notorious. Parading before the eyes of the masses the humiliation, subjection, deposition, and imprisonment of a lawful king was far more dangerous than declaring an offstage resignation. It was also explicitly requested by Meyrick when he paid Shakespeare's company a bonus of forty shillings to revive the play one last time. (It's doubtful the actors ever dared perform it again; and, indeed, the government suppressed an adaptation of the play as late as 1680.)

■ ■ ■

It was perhaps at about the same time as the Irish/Essex crisis in 1599 that various lines touching on Richard's career were removed from *Henry IV, Part 2*. Found in the Folio but missing from the quarto (published 1600) are four passages which were beginning, in light of recent events, to look a little suspicious. Though some are actually pro-Richard, any mention of the deposed king in connection with a fresh rebellion must have left the Master of Revels a bit queasy.

The first offender is a long speech by Morton, a minor anti-Henry rebel, reporting on the actions of a greater rebel, the Archbishop of York. York, Morton says, is urging on his followers "with the blood/ Of fair King Richard, scrap'd from Pomfret stones" (*2 Henry IV,* I.i.204–5). (Richard had been murdered, at Henry's request, at Pomfret Castle.) Talk of a usurped king's blood was bad enough, but it probably didn't help that one might find in York an allusion to Oviedo, a Spanish monk who was christened Bishop of Dublin and who, after the Essex fiasco, tried to incite further Irish uprisings.

A second missing passage stars the self-same Archbishop of York, who this time gloats over the rising popular tide against Henry IV, while at the same time reviling the fickleness of the masses:

O thou fond many, with what loud applause
Didst thou beat heaven with blessing Bolingbroke
Before he was what thou wouldst have him be!

And being now trimm'd in thine own desires,
Thou, beastly feeder, are so full of him,
That thou provok'st thyself to cast him up.
So, so, thou common dog, didst thou disgorge
Thy glutton bosom of the royal Richard,
And now thou wouldst eat thy dead vomit up,
And howl'st to find it. What trust is in these times?
They that, when Richard liv'd, would have him die,
Are now become enamor'd on his grave.
    [*With no small help from York!*—MM]
Thou, that threw'st dust upon his goodly head
When through proud London he came sighing on
After th' admired heels of Bolingbroke,
Cri'st now, "O earth, yield us that king again,
And take thou this!" O thoughts of men accurs'd!
Past and to come seems best; things present worst.

2 Henry IV, I.iii.91–108

The Archbishop should talk; in real life he had sided with Bolingbroke against Richard, only to turn rebel later when he began to be pinched by the new king's tax policies.

Third to go was York's justification of his rebellion (and
perhaps you're starting to notice that the edited play has big
gaps where a rebel leader used to be):

Wherefore do I do this? so the question stands.
Briefly, to this end: we are all diseas'd,
And with our surfeiting and wanton hours
Have brought ourselves into a burning fever,
And we must bleed for it; of which disease
Our late King Richard (being infected) died.

IV.i.53–58

York goes on to complain that he had earlier sought to discuss his grievances with King Henry, but was turned away. He and his fellows

> might by no suit gain our audience.
> When we are wrong'd and would unfold our griefs,
> We are denied access unto his person
> Even by those men that most have done us wrong.
>
> 76–79

It is interesting in this connection that Essex, too, was apparently steamed at being barred from the queen's presence. In fact, he would later claim that his rebellion was merely an attempt to barge his way back into it. So one can understand that York's espousing rebellion for being "denied access" might be viewed with some sensitivity.

Lastly, the quarto lacks a colloquy between Henry's man Westmoreland and the rebel Mowbray on a critical incident portrayed in *Richard II*. This was a feud between Bolingbroke (then Earl of Hereford) and Thomas Mowbray, Duke of Norfolk (and father of the rebel). Richard's bungling of this incident was the original cause of his subsequent overthrow by Bolingbroke. And as Westmoreland reports it, the people were even then behind Henry: "all their prayers and love/ Were set on Hereford, whom they doted on,/ And bless'd, and grac'd, indeed more than the King" (Arden, IV.i.135–37). If Queen Elizabeth saw herself as Richard II, Essex's supporters envisioned him as another Henry, whom they doted on far more than the queen.

▪ ▪ ▪

Shakespeare hit a few other snags in his dealings with the Revels Office. When we have multiple early texts of a play, suspicious material is often lacking from at least one of them. On the other hand, it may look suspicious just *because* it is lacking. When something's absence is our only evidence, it's tempting to invent sensational details.

For example, the Folio text of *Richard III* lacks a passage in which Richard explodes at his closest ally, Buckingham; the King has had enough of Buckingham's nagging demands for an earldom. Why it's missing is a mystery; Shakespeare may have cut it, or it may never have been in his original manuscript, which is the basis for the Folio text. But groundless speculation is more interesting, and some editors have theorized that the lines were struck because they offended King James, whose closest ally happened to be an unpopular social climber named Buckingham (a title doting James had bestowed). This scenario is not implausible; but neither is it substantiated.

Two other scenarios are more firmly grounded in evidence, though one is more fantastical. The first involves the failed script for a play to be known as *Sir Thomas More*. As you may recall, More was a Catholic martyr who lost his head to Henry VIII, father of the Virgin Queen. Such a figure required delicate handling—more delicate, it turns out, than the play's authors were capable of.

And there were many authors, probably as many as five: Anthony Munday, Henry Chettle, Thomas Dekker, possibly Thomas Heywood, and probably William Shakespeare. At what point in the process Shakespeare was enlisted is unknown; but it appears that in 1594 or '95 he contributed the scene in which More, then a sheriff of London, quells a xenophobic May Day riot. His speech is a patriotic homily that would warm the heart of any Tudor monarch. (More declares that God himself calls the King "a god on earth.")

But it evidently failed to sufficiently warm the Master of Revels, Sir Edmund Tilney. Perhaps even prior to Shakespeare's involvement, Tilney scribbled this note on the first page of the manuscript:

> Leave out the insurrection wholly & the cause thereof, & begin with Sir Thomas More at the mayor's sessions with a report afterwards of his good service done being the Shrive [sheriff] of London upon a mutiny against the Lumbards, only by a short report & not otherwise, at your own perils. E. Tilney.

If Shakespeare was hired to come up with a way to keep the insurrection while still pleasing Tilney, he failed. The play was rejected again, and may have been delivered a final blow around 1600, during the Essex crisis. In any case, *Sir Thomas More* would not be performed until 1964.

There is one more interesting case in Shakespeare's career of offending the powerful. But because its subject is so large, it requires a chapter of its own.

The Peculiar Case of Sir John Falstaff

▪

Perhaps the best loved, and certainly the most profane, of Shakespeare's characters is that fat knight Sir John Falstaff, who steals the show in both parts of *Henry IV* and in *The Merry Wives of Windsor.* Sir John is also a good example of how politics and religion were all mixed up in Shakespeare's day, and how touchy people could be about both.

Falstaff is bad. Very, very bad (see "God's Lid" and "Shakespeare's Lewd Lexicon," below). Which is also why he's so good. Not only is he funny, fun-loving, and full of life, he deflates the pomposities of a self-important political world. All the records show that audiences ate him up, eagerly returning to the theater, buying out the cheap editions of *1 Henry IV,* and clamoring for more. (At the end of *2 Henry IV,* Shakespeare promises we'll see even more of Sir John in *Henry V,* but it didn't quite work out that way.) Among Falstaff's fans was none other than Queen Elizabeth herself, who according to the legend commanded Shakespeare to whip up for her pleasure, in a mere two weeks, a play on Falstaff in love. Shakespeare obliged with the wry *Merry Wives.*

That tale, true or not, is well known. Less well known is the sensation Falstaff caused before his name was Falstaff. Those few who have read Shakespeare's first play, *Henry VI, Part 1* (ca. 1590), know it also features a certain "Sir John Falstaffe." This Falstaffe is based on the historical knight Sir John Fastolfe, who fought in the French wars of Henry VI. In 1429, Fastolfe withdrew from battle in Patay, near Orléans, for which he was temporarily branded a coward and expelled from the chivalric Order of the Garter.

History was kinder to Fastolfe than Shakespeare was. In real life, he was exonerated and restored to his glories; in *1 Henry VI,* his indignities are only multiplied. "Treacherous Falstaffe" not only flees from Patay, "not having struck one stroke" (I.i.134), he later turns tail at Rouen to save his own hide. He admits his own cowardice, and the hero Talbot removes his garter permanently.

A minor comic figure, Falstaffe was slated to become just another of Shakespeare's many forgotten characters. But then matters took a strange turn as the Bard was in the middle of chronicling earlier kings. His company had already staged *Richard II* and *Henry IV, Part 1;* the latter in particular was proving hugely popular, largely for the antics of a profane and dissolute knight named Sir John Oldcastle.

As Shakespeare was finishing a first sequel *(Henry IV, Part 2)* and plotting a second *(Henry V),* he continued to draw on various sources. Among them was an older play or plays published circa 1586 as *The Famous Victories of Henry the Fifth.* This is where the Bard had found Oldcastle, who plays a minor role in Prince Hal's riotous youth. Shakespeare saw real potential in the character, and built him up (quite unhistorically) into a towering figure of misrule, folly, vice, and irony. The combination was unbeatable.

But unless you're reading very closely, you won't find Oldcastle in either part of *Henry IV.* That is because by the time part 2 was acted, and before either was published,

"Oldcastle" had been changed to "Falstaff." We know this from contemporary testimony, and from telltale traces in the texts. But why was Shakespeare forced to revive the name of a cowardly knight from an earlier play and a different historical period? Because by transforming Oldcastle into a man of Herculean vices, Shakespeare angered the powerful, and jealous, descendants of a controversial historical figure.

The real Sir John Oldcastle (ca. 1375–1417) was a provincial bureaucrat who married into the title "Lord Cobham." He later fought in the French wars Shakespeare depicts in *Henry V* (where neither Oldcastle nor Falstaff appears). According to the chronicler Raphael Holinshed, a favorite Shakespeare source, Oldcastle was not only "a valiant captain and hardy gentleman," but also "highly in the king's favor." Unfortunately, he was also a Lollard, which is to say, a heretic.

Lollards, who held that religious authority lay in scripture and not in the dictates of a corrupt church, were zealously persecuted in the 14th and 15th centuries, not least in the days of Henry V. Oldcastle's favor with the king didn't save him from prosecution and conviction for heresy (after declaring the Pope the anti-Christ), but he managed to escape into hiding in Wales. Obviously, he wasn't available for any more expeditions to France, and his absence there may have led some to repute him a coward. In any case, at the end of 1417 he was captured, hanged, and burned.

Oldcastle's career would become a kind of politico-religious football in subsequent histories. Prior to the Reformation, he was excoriated and mocked in the chronicles, branded a degenerate, heretic, coward, and traitor, even an agent of Satan. It was also alleged that his intimacy with Henry predated the latter's reign—that is, that it was just one of the prince's youthful indiscretions. This version of events obviously found its way, through various channels, into Shakespeare's history plays.

But then in 1534 Henry VIII broke with the church, largely vindicating the Lollard cause. What was once called heresy was now viewed as valiant resistance to the corruptions and false teachings of Rome. Revisionists stepped forward to rehabilitate the martyrs to their cause, among them Oldcastle. In the Protestant version of his life, Oldcastle was not only a valiant and virtuous soldier, but also a spiritual philosopher and scholar who deeply inspired his fellow Lollards. It was admitted, however, that before his religious awakening he had been a bit rowdy in his youth.

Unfortunately for Oldcastle's latter-day champions, the Catholic version made for better plays. Shakespeare's dramatic instincts, rather than any Catholic sympathies, most likely shaped his Oldcastle. Among those not amused, it seems, was Sir William Brooke, Lord Cobham, who was not only Oldcastle's descendant but also lord chamberlain and thus one of the queen's closest advisers in 1596–97—precisely when *1 Henry IV* was first staged.

The evidence suggests that Brooke, angry at Shakespeare's portrait of his ancestor as a profane and riotous clown, demanded that the name be changed. (He may have demanded more, but a name change is what he got.) Brooke's intervention backfired, as the affair became the literary scandal of the season and a running joke. His successor, Henry Brooke, was dubbed "Sir John Falstaff" by witty rivals. A counter-play by four hacks, *The True and Honorable History of the Life of Sir John Oldcastle* (1599), appears to have bombed.

And Shakespeare got the last laugh. The queen herself must have been amused if she commanded a comedy featuring Oldcastle/Falstaff, and Shakespeare obliged with a play in which the fat knight is humiliated by the merry wives. And when the jealous fool Master Ford adopts an alias for his parleys with Falstaff, the name he goes by is "Master Brook." The younger Brooke must have taken this badly, as that name, too, is changed in later texts (to "Broom"), and at the end of *2 Henry IV* the Bard contritely admits that "Oldcastle died a martyr, and this [Falstaff] is not the man" (Epilogue.32).

This isn't the end of the story, however, for even the new name angered some people. This was the second time Shakespeare had sullied the reputation of the honorable Sir John Fastolfe, and it was more grist for the grievance mill. In 1625, a Dr. Richard James complained that on account of the Cobhams' objections, Shakespeare had been put "to make an ignorant shift of abusing Sir John Falstophe." The historian Thomas Fuller was more vehement in 1655:

> *Stage-Poets* have themselves been very *bold* with, and others very *merry* at, the Memory of Sir *John Oldcastle,* whom they have fancied a *boon Companion,* a *jovial Roister,* and yet a *Coward* to boot, contrary to the credit of all Chronicles, owning him a *Martial man* of merit. The best is, Sir *John Falstaff,* hath relieved the Memory of Sir *John Oldcastle,* and of late is substituted *Buffoon* in his place, but it matters little what *petulant Poets,* as what *malicious Papists* have written against him. (Arden, *1 Henry IV,* p. xvii)

Fuller would later amplify this, noting that "as I am glad that Sir *John Oldcastle* is *put out,* so I am sorry that Sir *John Fastolfe* is *put in*…to be an *anvil* for every *dull wit* to strike upon" (xvii–xviii). This was clearly a battle Shakespeare would never win, except, that is, among the public.

Saucy Priests and Nuns' Lips

Y ou wouldn't know it from reading Shakespeare, but Elizabethan England was a cauldron of religious paranoia. The Protestant establishment was, in its own mind, far from secure, threatened by recidivist Catholics on the one side and radical Puritans on the other. The Catholic threat was considered so grave that even private worship was outlawed, while harboring priests was declared a capital crime.

Given that the Crown's claim to absolute authority rested on its divine charter, the religious problem was as political as it was doctrinal. Religiously motivated intrigues, whether real or imagined, seemed as potentially ruinous as foreign armadas. Catholics at home and abroad were branded as dangerous enemies; and the nation trembled at tales of monkish plots to poison the queen.

But such exciting topics were off limits in the theater—which the authorities viewed as subversive enough as it was (see "Will's Naughty Theater," page 12). Besides, actors—whose status was slightly higher than vagabonds'—had no business dealing with God in the first place. Thus you won't find much in Shakespeare to suggest he had any religious beliefs at all—though some have perceived a subtle underlying sympathy with the outlawed Catholic cause.

Be that as it may, practically the only religious naughtiness in Shakespeare comes at Rome's expense. For one thing, it was relatively safe to pick on "papists"; and for another, many of his plays are set either in Catholic countries (e.g., Italy) or in England's Catholic past (all the histories, including *Henry VIII*, which takes place on the eve of the English Reformation). Some of the naughtiness is just traditional satire on corrupt clergymen; some (as in *King John*) is a direct attack on the hated Vatican and its agents.

A good example is Shakespeare's portrayal of Cardinal Wolsey in the late history *Henry VIII*. His highest ambition is not to serve the king, but rather to be Pope. A man of no real principle save self-interest, he continually dissembles his motives, grabbing power (and "piles of wealth") where he can.

Wolsey, whose heart is "cramm'd with arrogancy, spleen, and pride" (*Henry VIII,* II.iv.110), is also a dangerous enemy; he bribes witnesses to accuse his rival Buckingham of treason, for which the latter is executed. He's also instrumental in bringing down Henry's first queen, though shortly afterward his true nature is revealed, and he himself is condemned for treason, having "writ to th' Pope against the King" (III.ii.287).

Shakespeare's depiction of Wolsey isn't totally harsh—he allows the disgraced cardinal some dignity in the end. Nonetheless it distressed those of the Romish persuasion, in England and elsewhere, as it reinforced popular notions that the church had plotted—and continued to plot—against the

English crown. The antipapal invective in *King John* (sampled below) was even worse, and there are numerous scattered bits which would offend a faithful Catholic. While Shakespeare's works failed to make the Vatican's notorious Index of banned books, in the 1640s the Holy Office did endorse the effort of an English Jesuit living in Spain, William Sankey, to produce a censored version fit for Catholic consumption. Offensive epithets were cut, challenging speeches trimmed.

One play Father Sankey didn't like at all—and which he therefore removed altogether—was *Measure for Measure*. The reasons aren't hard to see; the plot features a would-be nun who winds up married to a duke, who himself has abdicated his office to spend most of the play masquerading as a Catholic friar. In this guise the duke blithely (and blasphemously) performs sacraments, while scheming to get an unmarried couple into bed. As he sees it, the ends justify all these dubious means, but that's not how the Vatican saw it.

What follows are further examples of passages offensive not only to Catholics but in some cases also to mainstream Protestants. It goes without saying that they offended Puritans and other radical sectarians, who hated plays from start to finish. I've excluded impious profanities (which are treated in the next chapter) and anti-Semitic jibes (which are also dealt with elsewhere—see page 101).

▪ Between illegally stealing the throne from his nephew and later capitulating to the Pope, King John gets his brief moment as a Protestant hero and symbolic precursor of Henry VIII. When John refuses to seat the Vatican's choice as Archbishop of Canterbury, he's challenged by the Pope's Machiavellian legate, Cardinal Pandulph, who repeats the demand "in our foresaid Holy Father's name,/ Pope Innocent" (*John*, III.i.145–46). Here's John's stinging reply, which would be "edited" by Sankey:

> Thou canst not, Cardinal, devise a name
> So slight, unworthy, and ridiculous,
> To charge me to an answer, as the Pope.
> Tell him this tale, and from the mouth of England
> Add thus much more, that no Italian priest
> Shall tithe or toll in our dominions;
> But as we, under God, are supreme head,

So under Him that great supremacy,
Where we do reign, we will alone uphold
Without th' assistance of a mortal hand.
So tell the Pope, all reverence set apart
To him and his usurp'd authority.

149–60

By invoking his "great supremacy," John unconsciously (but Shakespeare consciously) anticipates Henry VIII's Act of Supremacy, in which he declared himself supreme head of both English state and English church. (Henry's act stuck, but John's resolve will falter.)

After John makes a few more cutting remarks—calling the Pope a "meddling priest" and Catholic rites "juggling witchcraft" (163, 169)—Pandulph excommunicates him and then declares that whoever murders John will be "Canonized and worshipp'd as a saint" (177). Eventually John is poisoned by a monk.

■ On top of King John's epithets "Italian priest" and "meddlesome priest," Shakespeare piles more abuse on preachers and pastors. A central conflict in *Henry VI, Part 1* is the feud between the Duke of Gloucester and the Bishop of Winchester, both of whom hope to control the child king. Gloucester's rhetoric is poisonously harsh: Winchester is a "Peel'd [shaved, tonsured] priest," a "manifest conspirator" that "giv'st whores indulgences to sin"—a reference both to the Bishop's profit from brothels in London's Bankside district and to the church's sale of "indulgences" or absolutions (*1 Henry VI*, I.iii.30–35). When Winchester "beards" Gloucester "to [his] face"—i.e., openly defies him, Gloucester sputters,

What? am I dar'd and bearded to my face?
.... Priest, beware your beard,
I mean to tug it and to cuff you soundly.
Under my feet I stamp thy cardinal's hat;
In spite of Pope or dignities of church,
Here by the cheeks I'll drag thee up and down.

I.iii.45–51

Later, Gloucester calls Winchester a "Presumptuous priest" (III.i.8), a "most pernicious usurer" (17), "Lascivious" and "wanton" (19), a "bastard" (42), and a "saucy priest" (45).

■ Winchester, a.k.a. Beauford, comes in for more drubbing in *Henry VI, Part 2*. The Earl of Salisbury notes that he has seen "the haughty Cardinal,... As stout and proud as he were lord of all,/ Swear like a ruffian, and demean himself" (*2 Henry VI*, I.i.185–88). Gloucester's wife calls him "impious Beauford, that false priest" (II.iv.53); but she has little room to talk, as she had eagerly joined two "priests" in conjuring up a satanic "Spirit" (I.iv). Meanwhile, the Queen rails on her monkish husband:

I thought King Henry had resembled thee [her lover
......Suffolk]
In courage, courtship, and proportion;
But all his mind is bent to holiness,
To number Ave-Maries on his beads;
His champions are the prophets and apostles,
His weapons holy saws of sacred writ,
His study is his tilt-yard, and his loves
Are brazen images of canonized saints.
I would the college of the Cardinals
Would choose him Pope and carry him to Rome,

And set the triple crown on his head—
That were a state fit for his holiness.

I.iii.53–64

Though she's a wicked, scheming Frenchwoman, Margaret is correct about Henry's idolatrous papistical devotion, which makes him a weak and credulous king.

■ Neither Frenchmen nor Catholics were likely to be gratified by Shakespeare's depiction of Joan of Arc, in *1 Henry VI,* not as a saint, but as a slut and a witch.

■ When Henry VIII severed the English church from Rome, he also seized a great deal of property formerly held by monasteries or used for income rather than worship. Seizures of this sort had been attempted before in a series of failed parliamentary bills. At the beginning of *Henry V,* the Archbishop of Canterbury and the Bishop of Ely worry over the latest attempt of Parliament to take "the better half of our [income-generating] possession" and to use it to expand the gentry and to build leper houses and almshouses (I.i.7–19). Scheming over how to prevent such a disaster, they agree on a course of action: urge war against France and then help pay the bill. This will distract both king and Parliament, and justify the church's profits. The plan succeeds, and by the end of the play thousands (mostly French) have died in battle.

■ The religious situation in *Hamlet* is (like most things about the play) incredibly tangled. The ghost of Hamlet's murdered father complains that he died "Unhous'led, disappointed, unanel'd" (*Hamlet,* I.v.77), terms which refer to Catholic sacraments, and he seems to be currently residing in Purgatory, which Protestants dismissed as a popish fantasy. (Protestants as well as Catholics, however, believed in ghosts, spirits, and witchcraft.) Denmark had long been a Protestant country. In any case, when the (seemingly Protestant) "Doctor of Divinity" who oversees Ophelia's burial treats her death as a suicide (see page 35), her brother Laertes calls him "churlish priest" and vows that "A minist'ring angel shall my sister be/ When thou liest howling" (V.i.240–42).

■ In *The Merry Wives of Windsor,* the enraged Frenchman Dr. Caius (a Catholic?) calls the Welsh parson Sir Hugh Evans (definitely Protestant) "a scurvy jack-a-nape priest" (*Wives,* I.iv.109–10), "de Jack priest" (117), and "de coward Jack priest" (II.iii.31). "Jack" is "a term of contempt for saucy and paltry, or silly fellows" (Schmidt); "jack-a-nape" means "coxcomb" or "monkey."

■ When Aaron the evil Moor is brought with his blackamoor bastard to Lucius, the righteous son of Titus Andronicus, Aaron observes, "I know thou art religious,/ And hast a thing within thee called conscience,/ With twenty popish tricks and ceremonies,/ Which I have seen thee careful to observe" (*Titus,* V.i.74–77). Given that the play is set in pagan Rome (where human sacrifice is a matter of course), Aaron is a little off-base with "popish"; but Shakespeare's audience would have understood the slur. On the other hand, given that Aaron is an atheist, it isn't necessarily to the Pope's discredit.

■ Lest we forget Father Sankey, there are several other quasi-blasphemous lines he saw fit to remove. For example, he didn't like the King of Navarre's invocation of "Saint Cupid" on the heels of Berowne's biblical discourse in *Love's*

Labor's Lost (IV.iii.363). The Princess of France also yokes "Saint" to the pagan god (V.ii.87), and that was cut, too.

▪ Not only Sankey but also some squeamish editors of the 18th century took exception to one of Rosalind's metaphors in *As You Like It*. Singing the praises of her heartthrob Orlando, she gushes that "his kissing is as full of sanctity as the touch of holy bread" (*AYL*, III.iv.13–14). Most glossers distinguish "holy bread" from the even more sacred Eucharist wafer, but the distinction isn't apparent in context, and in any case many have been offended. In his 1747 edition of Shakespeare, John Warburton changed "bread" to "beard," claiming that the Bard really meant "the kiss of a holy saint or hermit."

▪ In *All's Well That Ends Well*, the Clown claims to have "an answer will serve all men," that is, one answer to fit any question. It is a fit as "the nail to his hole, the cuckold to his horn," and a panoply of other matches (see page 171), including this: "as the nun's lip to the friar's mouth" (*AWW*, II.ii.13–14, 24–27). This bawdy satire on the secret passions of the supposedly abstinent Catholic clergy prompted Sankey to pull out his eraser.

"God's Lid" and Other Offensive Oaths

For most of Shakespeare's career, the government limited the content of stage plays. As we saw in "Will's Naughty Theater" (page 12), the Master of Revels would examine scripts for offensive subjects, and send them back for rewriting if he found any. But he never checked the bawdy scenes or double-entendres; in fact, he left Shakespeare's language pretty well alone.

That changed in 1606 with the Act to Restrain Abuses of Players, which prohibited certain profanities in performance or print. The list did not include "whore," or "codpiece," or "pillicock," or any of the other members of "Shakespeare's Lewd Lexicon" (page 181). It more narrowly focused on far more offensive terms—terms far more potent than a modern audience can appreciate—namely, oaths that profaned "the holy Name of God" (or one of His aliases).

Shakespeare is admittedly pretty loose in this area, especially when "foul-mouth'd" Falstaff or "swaggering" Pistol is onstage. After 1606 he restrained himself, but his older work was still in circulation, and it was full of impious jests and profanities. Fortunately, when it came to new editions of moldy old plays, the Master of Revels was lenient. Or had been more lenient, until a new and more puritanical master took office even as compositors were setting type for Shakespeare's famous First Folio of 1623.

Informed of the new regime's stricter policy, the Folio editors hastily set about cleaning up the histories and tragedies. But the comedies had already been printed, and the publisher was damned if he was going to eat those costs. (Someone must have worked out a compromise with the Revels Office.) As a result, the comedies emerged unscathed while the rest were cleansed.

On the other hand, whoever was in charge of censoring oaths did a haphazard job. He managed to catch and censor every occurrence of the very offensive "'zounds" (short for "God's wounds"). On the other hand, less outrageous oaths such as "in faith" and "God help me" are cut here and left alone there. And the shocking "God's lid" survives in the Folio version of *Troilus and Cressida,* which is classed as a tragedy. I explore the checkered results of censoring *Henry IV, Part 1* in the next chapter.

Later editors would prove far more efficient. Thomas Bowdler, for example, expunged every last "God's lid" from his *Family Edition* of Shakespeare (see page 20). Like his Jacobean predecessors, he supplied innocuous substitutions where possible ("by God" becomes "by Heaven"), and deleted where it wasn't. Modern editors usually take the opposite course, by restoring the Folio's cuts. So most of the editions in print today are more profane than the Folio.

The following is a sampling of Shakespeare's censored oaths. (Cross-references are set in SMALL CAPITALS.) To keep the list to a manageable size, I'll pass over such milder oaths as "God's mercy" and "for God's sake," which are numerous. You'll notice that a few plays (such as *Othello* and both parts of *Henry IV*) are especially offensive. They are best avoided.

GOD'S BLESSING ON YOUR BEARD!

Longaville, *Love's Labor's Lost,* II.i.203

Apparently a very sharp comeback, though more for the "beard" than the "God." In those days, male facial hair was a point of pride, and "to play with someone's beard" was to insult him. Insult is clearly Longaville's point; so one wonders where God's blessing comes into it. Most likely, Longaville is just stringing together the oaths that occur to him.

GOD'S BODY

1 Carrier, *1 Henry IV,* II.i.26

Swearing by Christ's body (or any part thereof) was off limits in civil discourse. Characters who do so are either very angry or just coarse. The carrier is just coarse (he's the Renaissance equivalent of a trucker).

GOD'S BODYKINS, MAN

Hamlet, *Hamlet,* II.ii.529

Sometimes spelled *bodkin,* the word means "little body" or "dear body." (Using diminutives is often a sign of endearment.) We're never told why Hamlet swears in the plural, but that seems to be standard; Shallow had already cried "Bodykins, Master Page" in *Merry Wives* (II.iii.44). Singular or plural, the cute suffix doesn't make the oath acceptable. Alexander Schmidt calls it "scurrilous" in his *Shakespeare Lexicon and Quotation Dictionary.*

OD'S HEARTLINGS

Slender, *Wives,* III.iv.57

A variation on the theme of *bodykins,* this means "God's little hearts." If the phrase refers to Christ, he only had one; but by shrinking it and multiplying it, you almost can't tell you're swearing on it. Whoever edited the Folio left the phrase alone, although he changed "I thank God" to "I thank heaven" a single line later.

BY GOD'S LID

Pandarus, *Troilus and Cressida,* I.ii.211

"By God's eyelid," judged a "mild oath" by *Riverside.* But compare 'SLID, below.

OD'S LIFELINGS!

Sir Andrew Aguecheek, *Twelfth Night,* V.i.184

Either "God's little lives," or "God save [our] little lives." Though the latter seems like a stretch, see OD'S MY LITTLE LIFE, below.

BY GOD'S LIGGENS

Justice Shallow, *2 Henry IV,* V.iii.65

Whatever it means, the censors didn't like it. A. R. Humphreys, editor of the Arden edition, thinks *liggens* may be another diminutive form, perhaps a corruption of *lidkins,* or "little lids." See BY GOD'S LID and 'SLID.

BY GOD'S [BLEST] MOTHER!

Three occurrences: Gloucester, *2 Henry VI,* II.i; King Edward, *3 Henry VI,* III.ii; King Henry, *Henry VIII,* V.i.

Swearing by the Virgin is almost as bad as swearing by her Son. Especially when, like Gloucester, you're addressing a Catholic Cardinal.

OD'S MY LITTLE LIFE

Rosalind, *As You Like It,* III.v.43

This clearly means "God save my little life," a diminution of "God's my life" (found twice in Shakespeare). It's not too far a stretch from *little life* to *lifelings,* noted above.

OD'S MY WILL

Rosalind, *AYL,* IV.iii.17

"God's my will," a pious sentiment that pulls the punch of using His name in vain. As with OD'S MY LITTLE LIFE (above), Rosalind is attempting to swear like a man as part of her pretense that she is one. Though they're certainly not the kinds of things a proper young lady would say, they're not especially hard-hitting, either. Shakespeare holds her to the fair side of virtue, at some expense to her credibility; but that's not such a problem for an audience already willing to accept fair Rosalind as acted by a boy.

A' GOD'S NAME!

Ten occurrences: Charles the Dolphin, *1 Henry VI,* I.ii; King Henry, *2 Henry VI,* II.iii; Jack Cade, *2 Henry VI,* IV.vii; Willoughby, *Richard II,* II.i; King Richard, *Richard II,* III.iii; Hastings, *Richard III,* III.iv; Buckingham, *Henry VIII,* II.i; Gremio, *Shrew,* I.ii; Petruchio, *Shrew,* IV.v; Benedick, *Much Ado,* I.i.

"In the name of God!" A bit rougher than "For God's sake," and it tends to be spoken in moments of passion. The Dolphin (crown prince of France) aims it at Joan of Arc, and Benedick at his equally fierce nemesis Beatrice. When fully articulated as "In God's name" it's more restrained, and about as serious as "For God's sake."

OD'S NOUNS

Mistress Quickly, *Wives,* IV.i.24

> The lady isn't swearing on a part of speech; this is another
> slurred version of "God's wounds" (see 'ZOUNDS, below).

BE GOD'S SONTIES!

Old Gobbo, *Merchant,* II.ii.45

> Perhaps meaning "By God's little saints," this is a garbled
> version of the already obscure "By God's santy," which
> first appears in 1570. Old Gobbo is as profane as his son,
> who has just uttered the extremely familiar but still un-
> suitable "marry," a corruption of the Virgin's name.

OD'S PLESSED WILL!

Evans, *Wives,* I.i.264

> "Blessed" in Evans's crippled enunciation. On a par with
> Rosalind's OD'S MY WILL (above).

UD'S PITY

Emilia, *Othello,* IV.iii.75

> A particularly ugly corruption of "God's pity," the phrase
> is censored in the Folio and replaced with a feeble "why."

OD'S PITTIKINS

Imogen, *Cymbeline,* IV.ii.293

> Like Rosalind (see OD'S MY WILL, above), Imogen disguises
> herself as a male youth, and then belts out this little curse to
> strengthen the act. It's "Ud's pity" with all the edge shaved off.

GOD-I-GODEN

Capulet, *Romeo,* III.v.172

Irate old Capulet sputters out this oath when Juliet resists his plans for her marriage. Spelled "goddegodden" in the earliest text, it is perhaps a heavily slurred version of "God in the good evening." Even so, it doesn't really *mean* anything; it just signifies pique.

GOD'S BREAD, IT MAKES ME MAD!

Capulet, *Romeo,* III.v.176

Capulet, even madder, uncorks this one four lines after God-i-goden. It may refer to the sacramental bread of Communion—which stands for God's body—or it may be meaningless. Along with oaths like "God's lid," it's probably less a phrase to be analyzed than a phrase to just deplore.

BY CHESU

Fluellen (four times), *Henry V,* III.ii.63, 70, 79, and 83

BY CHRISH

Macmorris (twice), *Henry V,* III.ii.88 and 109

SO CHRISH SAVE ME

Macmorris (four times), *Henry V,* III.ii.92, 105, 113, and 133

"Chesu" and "Chrish" are "Jesus" and "Christ," respectively, in Fluellen's Welsh accent and Macmorris's Irish. Such expletives aren't surprising in a bluff exchange among soldiers. But they (and Macmorris's "So God sa' me" at line 110) should have been cut somewhere along the line, and they never were. It's possible that this whole scene was pasted in after the play was first passed by the Master of Revels. According to one theory (Arden), the scene was added to replace another comic interlude starring Falstaff, who was forced out of the play by political pressure (see page 66).

IN THE NAME OF JESU CHRIST

Fluellen, *Henry V,* IV.i.65

The censors missed this one, and somebody else missed the fact that Fluellen is supposed to say "Chesu."

BY JESU

Mercutio, *Romeo,* II.iv.29–31

Mercutio mimics the swaggering speech of the preening gallant Tybalt: "By Jesu, a very good blade! a very tall man! a very good whore!" This is the quintessence of what the censors were looking for, but *Romeo* appears to have passed unchecked. Compare the zeal with which they hunted down "O Jesu" in the two parts of *Henry IV,* where all six occurrences are cut. (A pious "Jesus bless us!" is allowed to stand at *1 Henry IV,* II.ii.82.)

BY THE MASS

Counting the shorter "Mass," this oath appears 23 times: in *Much Ado* (twice), *Wives, 1 Henry IV* (twice), *2 Henry IV* (seven times), *Henry V* (three times, counting Jamy's "mess" and a "mass" cut from the Folio), *2 Henry VI* (three times), *Romeo, Hamlet* (three times), and *Othello.*

Just serious enough to be cut or changed ten times in the later texts. This profanation of the holy sacrament is especially favored by Justice Shallow in *2 Henry IV.* (The Henriad is a problem, as usual.)

'ZOUNDS!

Twenty-three occurrences, ten of them in *1 Henry IV.* The rest appear in *Titus* (once), *Richard III* (four times), *Romeo* (twice), and *Othello* (six times). Iago and Falstaff are the worst offenders.

It may seem amusing to us now, but this oath—short for "God's wounds"—was strong stuff in Shakespeare's day. Iago, in his campaign to enrage Brabantio, lets it fly twice; and we know Othello's really far gone by the time he blurts it out too. References to the wounds or blood of God were thought especially outrageous, as they touched directly on the Crucifixion, which is beyond the pale of street talk. With only a single exception in *King John* (II.i.466), it's always censored in the Folio—usually by simple deletion, but sometimes by substitution. The replacements are as banal as can be—words like "out" and "what" and "come"; only Hotspur, with "By this hand," gets anything remotely interesting to say instead (*1 Henry IV,* II.iii.22).

'SBLOOD

Twelve occurrences: eight times in *1 Henry IV* (with Falstaff accounting for six), plus once in *Henry V,* twice in *Hamlet,* and once in *Othello.*

Less frequent than "'Zounds," this is the other really bad one, for identical reasons. And it's likewise expunged from the Folio (with a slip at *Henry V,* IV.viii.10). A few novel words are used in its place, including "away" and "yfaith." For some reason Falstaff, the most profane of Shakespeare's characters, is less corrosive in the sequel, *2 Henry IV,* even though that play still had to be plenty cleaned up for the Folio.

'SLID

Slender, *Wives,* III.iv.24; Sir Andrew Aguecheek, *Twelfth Night,* III.iv.391

In Schmidt's view, "a mean oath, used by such persons as Mr. Slender and Sir Andrew, corrupted from *God's lid.*"

'SLIGHT

Sir Andrew Aguecheek, *Twelfth Night,* II.v.33 and III.ii.13

A slight little curse, indeed, meaning "God's light." The mean Sir Andrew uses it in a vaguely threatening way, as in "'Slight! will you make an ass o' me?" Too harmless to bother censoring.

'SWOUNDS

Hamlet, *Hamlet,* II.ii.576 and V.i.274

As we might expect from the Prince, a slightly more articulate version of "'Zounds." Nonetheless, it was replaced by "why" and "come," respectively. Also censored in some earlier texts.

Censors at Work

■

By now, you should have an idea of what the speech police found objectionable. Now let's take a look at how Shakespeare's editors managed to improve a randomly chosen play—say, *Henry IV, Part 1*. Here's a list of words or phrases found in an early text, the "First Quarto" (1598), but omitted from a later one, the First Folio (1623). The Folio is the original and official collection of Shakespeare's works, published seven years after his death. But the quarto is thought to be close to Shakespeare's manuscript.

Unless otherwise noted, the listed phrases were simply removed from the text. It's a good thing the play is largely in prose.

scene   censored text (line number)

I.ii   by my troth (20)
          By the Lord (39)
          'Sblood (73)
          to God (82)
          wisdom cries out in the streets, and no man regards it (88) [an irreverent quotation from Proverbs, and irreverently quoting the Bible was definitely out]
          'Zounds (100)
          by my faith (138)
          By the Lord (146)
          God give thee (152) ["Mayest thou have" in the Folio]
          holy-days (204) ["holidays"]

I.iii   holy-day (46) ["holiday"]
'Zounds (131) ["Yes"]
god-night (194) ["good night"]
God (214) ["heaven"]
'Sblood (247)
i' faith (258) ["in sooth"]

II.i   by the mass (16)
king christen (17) ["king in Christendom"; "christen" is a
    slurred form of "Christian"]
God's body (26)
by God (36) ["I pray ye"]
'zounds (79)
by my faith (88)

II.ii   'Sblood (35)
'Zounds (65)

II.iii   By the Lord (16) ["I protest"]
'Zounds (22) ["By this hand"]
faith (79) ["sooth"]
In faith (87) ["Indeed"]

II.iv   salvation (9) ["confidence"]
by the Lord (13)
I could sing psalms, or any thing (133–34) ["I could sing all
    manner of songs"; this is another objectionable reference
    to the Bible]
'Zounds (144)
by the Lord (145)
God (189) ["Heaven"]
'Zounds (236) ["No"]
'Sblood (244) ["Away"]
By the Lord (267)

by the Lord (275)
O Jesu (284)
Faith (303)
i' faith (371)
O Jesu (390)
Jesu (395) ["rare"]
'Sblood (443) ["Yfaith"—which is, ironically, an alternate
    spelling of "i' faith"]
i' faith (444)
God (470) ["Heaven"]
Jesu (486)
God night (523) ["Good night"]
god morrow (524) ["good morrow"]

III.i   Heart (247) [short for "God's heart" and thus cut]

III.ii   God (4) ["Heaven"]
God (29) ["Heaven"]
God (130) ["Heaven"]
God (153) ["Heaven"]

III.iii   that's God's angel (35)
God (48) ["Heaven"]
'Sblood (49)
God-a-mercy (50)
God's light (62)
O Jesu (83)
'Sblood (86)
i' faith (88)
God (117) ["Heaven"]
God (118) ["Heaven"]
I pray God (151) ["let"]

IV.i   God (6) ["Heaven"]
          'Zounds (17)

IV.iii   God (38) ["Heaven"]
          God (113) ["Heaven"]

V.i   God (126) ["Heaven"]

V.iii   God (34) ["Heaven"]
          before God (50)

V.iv   God (11) ["Heaven"]
          God's (16) ["Heaven's"]
          God (17) ["Heaven"]
          God (51) ["Heaven"]
          God (69) ["Heaven"]
          'Sblood (113)
          'Zounds (121)
          By my faith (123)
          'zounds (152)
          God (163) ["Heaven"]

As you can see, the censor had his hands full, so it's not surprising that he didn't catch everything. His work, however, is *so* inconsistent that one wonders whether his heart was really in the job. For example, Falstaff's "By the mass" escapes the blade (II.iv.364), even though the phrase is cut from an earlier scene (II.i) and from other texts in the Folio (such as *2 Henry IV*). At least fifteen profane uses of "God" remain, including Hotspur's shocking "God's me!" at II.iii.95, as well as several uses of "in faith," a "Jesus bless us," and a "Lord, Lord."

Racist, Anti-Semite, Xenophobe?

W e'd all like to think that gentle Shakespeare hadn't an in-
tolerant bone in his body. But we must also admit that
"Otherness," to use the fashionable term, gets little respect in his plays, which are dotted with racial epithets and
other ugly sentiments. Some of the most offensive slurs are uttered by villains, which might lead us to suppose the Bard dis-
approved. But there's more than enough abuse to go around;
the good guys can be just as nasty as the bad.

Shakespeare's business was to imitate life, not to deliver
sermons. Since the characters speak for themselves, we must
pass our own judgments. The Bard may or may not have
agreed with Othello that the Turks were "dogs"; we don't
know, and it's impossible to calculate his precise attitude. But
that he puts such lines in his characters' mouths at least displays a certain insensitivity.

If he'd been more careful, Shakespeare could have avoided
much embarrassment. In our more enlightened age we require
explanations and apologies from authors who employ or quote
racial slurs; they must prove that they don't really *mean* them
(since readers can't decide for themselves). Mark Twain failed
to do so in *Huckleberry Finn,* and look what's happened to
him. T. S. Eliot did put some distance between himself and the
apparent anti-Semitism of certain prewar writings; but it was
too little, too late for today's arbiters of moral purity. Shakespeare offers no explanations and no apologies, which has left
him wide open to critical attack. It certainly hasn't helped his

cause when it comes to assembling syllabi, though so far as I know he hasn't yet been banned from any public library. It may only be a matter of time.

With all due respect to those who find prejudice painful, I think we may be losing our historical perspective. One of the triumphs of Shakespeare's age was to begin appreciating the distances and differences between past and present, and also among cultures. One needn't approve the attitudes of the past, but one should at least be able to respect their difference from our own. Shakespeare is *not* our contemporary; we should neither justify reading his work for its "relevance," nor condemn it for failing to ratify our own prejudices.

Was Shakespeare a racist, an anti-Semite, and a xenophobe? It's vain to seek an answer, for two reasons. First, his personal opinions are as opaque on Otherness as they are on practically everything else—his characters are his characters, not surrogate Shakespeares. Second, terms like "racism" depend on standards and judgments peculiar to particular times and places; they can't measure the same thing across the space of four hundred years as they measure today.

Certainly, some of Shakespeare's characters are prejudiced; even the black Othello hates the color of his skin. It's stupid to pretend that the prejudices aren't there. But what such sentiments mean should be considered with respect to his time, not ours. We need to read more of Shakespeare's and his contemporaries' works, not less, if we're going to understand their attitudes, rather than simply dismissing them.

Racism

In Shakespeare, black is anything but beautiful. Indeed, "black" is the most common antonym for "fair," a word equating beauty with whiteness. A pallid complexion was thought highly attractive in those days, partly because it was rare and required cultivation—only the very wealthy could afford to keep their sons, daughters, and wives entirely out of the sun.

A "black" or dark complexion, contrarily, was most definitely a turn-off—a "foul blot" made by erring Nature (*Much Ado,* III.i.64). Only lovesick fools praise a dark skin; besotted with his Dark Lady, Shakespeare denies the obvious: "I have sworn thee fair, and thought thee bright," he confesses, "Who art as black as hell, and dark as night" (*Sonnets,* 147.13–14). Detached observers usually react much like King Ferdinand, who observes that "Black is the badge of hell,/ The hue of dungeons, and the school of night" (*Love's Labor's Lost,* IV.iii.250–51).

Ferdinand refers merely to a dark-complexioned brunette; as you can imagine, Africans—called Ethiops or Moors in Shakespeare—get it even worse. What Shakespeare personally knew about Africans would probably have fit in a thimble, but that never stopped him before. Sometimes his characters merely use "Ethiop" as the superlative form of "ugly," as in Proteus's reflection that "Sylvia (witness heaven, that made her fair)/ Shows Julia but a swarthy Ethiop" (*Two Gentlemen,* II.vi.25–26). In other cases, they're more directly racist, as when Roderigo calls Othello "the thick-lips" (*Othello,* I.i.66), or refers to the "gross clasps of a lascivious Moor" (126).

Speaking of *Othello,* you might reasonably think that its portrayal of the title character, Roderigo's "Moor," refutes any charge that Shakespeare was racist. And you would have a good point, for Othello is (at first) a brave and noble general whose capabilities have propelled him to a top spot in the

Venetian military. The idea would not have been strange to an Elizabethan, as the Moors had come to England's aid against their mutual enemy, Catholic Spain. So Moors, while strange, ugly, and somewhat savage, could also be heroic, romantic, and generous—three qualities initially present in Shakespeare's exotic hero. We can be sure that Richard Burbage, the company's leading actor, cut an impressive and charismatic figure, even in blackface.

But the message of *Othello* is mixed at best. It's true that Othello has earned ungrudging respect from most of his peers and from the state, most recently by successfully opposing the despised Turks (see "Ethnic Insensitivity," page 107). But he commits a very big blunder when he crosses the color line to marry the fair Desdemona, daughter of a Venetian senator. Practically everyone aside from the newlyweds—including and especially Desdemona's father, Brabantio—finds the match improbable if not grotesque and incredible. Though all admire Othello for his military skill and courage, no Venetian wants his daughter to marry a Moor. Brabantio, in fact, literally dies from the shame.

Brabantio wasn't the last to be shocked. A number of latter-day critics were, too, and some of them even denied that Othello is black. S. T. Coleridge, for example, insisted that "It would be something monstrous to conceive this beautiful Venetian girl falling in love with a veritable negro," which would "argue a disproportionateness, a want of balance, in Desdemona." But as M. R. Ridley notes in the Arden edition of *Othello,* "that is precisely what, in the opinion of observers, it *does* argue, and what, for the right appreciation of the two characters concerned…it *should* argue" (p. liii). Othello *is* a "veritable negro," the marriage *is* shocking, and Desdemona *will* regret it.

The most racist characters in the play—Iago, Roderigo, and Brabantio—are far from admirable. But by the end we hate Othello more than anyone except perhaps Iago, his treacherous seducer. Of all Shakespeare's tragic "heroes," including Macbeth, Othello is the most despicable; and though Iago drives him to his crimes, his race also has something to do with them. The interracial marriage is a disaster waiting to happen; however valiant and however Westernized he may be, Othello still can't grasp the mores and mentality of his adopted culture. He himself doubts that he understands, or knows how to cope with, a white wife.

Desdemona falls in love with Othello despite, not because of, his race. She's captivated by his exploits and by the marvelous tales he spins; "I saw Othello's visage in his mind," she explains (*Othello,* I.iii.252). That is, she sees past his abhorrent appearance to his true interior character. The problem is that Othello's "mind" is at best a blunt instrument, easily mastered by the subtle and resentful Iago. Iago accurately measures Othello's insecurity and credulity; but he may underestimate Desdemona when he tells Roderigo that the Moor must eventually disgust her:

Her eye must be fed; and what delight shall she have to look on the devil? When the blood is made dull with the act of sport [sex], there should be, again to inflame it and to give satiety a fresh appetite, loveliness in favor [face], sympathy in years, manners, and beauties—all which the Moor is defective in. Now for want of these requir'd conveniences, her delicate tenderness will find itself abus'd, begin to heave the gorge, disrelish and abhor the Moor; very nature will instruct her in it and compel her to some second choice.

II.i.225–35

Whether or not Iago is correct, so far Othello's blackness hasn't heaved his wife's gorge. If anything, the exotic tension between his color and his character only enhances his appeal to Desdemona. Nevertheless, it does not cancel out what he calls his "begrim'd and black" complexion (III.iii.387).

Shakespeare is fond of exploring the boundaries between appearance and reality, seeming and being, testing whether the difference between them is itself merely apparent. Unfortunately for Othello, his reality has more to do with his appearance than he fancies. His inner qualities do not make him "white," despite Desdemona's wishes to the contrary. In the view of the play, Othello, as an African, is intellectually and emotionally simpler than the Venetians; and he has a shorter distance to fall into barbarity. David Garrick, a successful producer and actor who staged *Othello* in the mid-18th century, explained it this way:

[Shakespeare] had shown us white men jealous in other pieces, but that their jealousy had limits, and was not so terrible.… [In] Othello, he had wished to paint that passion in all its violence, and that is why he chose an African in whose being circulated fire instead of blood, and whose true or imaginary character could excuse all boldness of expression and all exaggerations of passion. (Rosenberg, 40)

Garrick certainly has a point; as a Moor, Shakespeare's tragic hero is both out of place in white society and less emotionally "restrained." (Another critic referred to "the impetuous ferocity natural to one of Othello's complexion.") And thus the marriage of black and white leads, with Iago's help, to a bloody conclusion: Desdemona's murder and Othello's suicide.

You couldn't call this a positive racial message. On the other hand, Shakespeare's manifest ambivalence in *Othello* is at least an improvement on the sentiments usually expressed by his characters. To the degree Othello is admirable, he's exceptional; and to the degree we admire him, we rise above the usual Renaissance view of the African character, which is often reduced to skin color. From his earliest to his latest plays, Shakespeare uses *black, Moor, Ethiop,* and other such terms mostly for abuse:

■ On Tamora's affair with Aaron the Moor, Bassianus remarks, "Believe me, Queen, your swart Cimmerian/ Doth make your honor of his body's hue,/ Spotted, detested, and abominable" (*Titus Andronicus,* II.iii.72–74). "Swart" means "swarthy, dark-skinned," and "Cimmerians" are quasi-mythical denizens of a land of darkness—a misconception, of course, since Africa is sunnier than Europe. Other epithets for Aaron include "barbarous Moor," "coal-black Moor," "irreligious Moor," "misbelieving Moor," and "damned Moor."

■ When Titus upbraids his brother for killing a fly, Marcus replies, "Pardon me, sir, it was a black ill-favor'd fly,/ Like to the Empress' Moor, therefore I kill'd him (*Titus,* III.ii.66–67).

■ When Tamora gives birth to a "blackamoor" child, the nursemaid calls it "loathsome as a toad/ Amongst the fair-fac'd breeders of our clime" (*Titus,* IV.ii.67–68). "'Zounds,

ye whore," Aaron curses, "is black so base a hue?" (71). To
Aaron the baby is his "thick-lipp'd slave" (175); to Lucius, it's
the "growing image of thy fiend-like face" (V.i.45).

■ Spurning the woman who loves him, the brunette Hermia,
Lysander cries, "Away, you Ethiop!" (*MND*, III.ii.257), and
then, "Out, tawny Tartar, out!" (263). (Tartars, Eurasian relatives of the Turks, were so called by association of their
own name, *Tatar*, with the Latin *Tartarus*, "hell.")

■ When she hears that the Prince of Morocco comes courting,
Portia blanches: "If he have the condition [character] of a
saint, and the complexion of a devil, I had rather he should
shrive me than wive me" (*The Merchant of Venice*,
I.ii.129–31). And while she tells him in person that she doesn't
at all mind his looks, when he fails the test for her hand she
heaves a sigh of relief: "A gentle riddance. Draw the cur-
tains, go./ Let all of his complexion choose me so"—i.e., fail
to win me (II.vii.78–79).

■ The first scene of *Othello* is full of incendiary racial slurs.
Roderigo calls the Moor "thick-lips" (I.i.66). To stir up Brabantio, Iago shouts out that "Even now, now, very now, an
old black ram/ Is tupping your white ewe" (88–89)—the
"ewe" being Brabantio's lily-white daughter, Desdemona.
Continuing his beastly metaphor, Iago asserts that Desdemona's being "cover'd with a Barbary [North African]
horse," and that the pair are "making the beast with two
backs" (111–17). Roderigo sings harmony, conjuring up the
"gross clasps of a lascivious Moor" (126). In the following
scene, Brabantio accosts Othello in the street and demands
to know how his daughter, who's refused the suits of
Venice's "wealthy curled darlings," could be drawn to "the
sooty bosom/ Of such a thing as thou" (I.ii.70–71).

■ In *Richard II,* Carlisle sings a paean to the Duke of Norfolk, a valiant soldier in the Crusades, who flies the Christian flag "Against black pagans, Turks, and Saracens" (IV.i.95). "Black pagans" are African Muslims; on the Turks, see below.

■ Caliban, whose name is an anagram of "cannibal," is also rather obviously a person of color. Prospero calls him a "thing of darkness" (*The Tempest,* V.i.275), while others label him a "moon-calf [monstrosity]" (II.ii.106), a "most scurvy monster" (155), an "abominable monster" (159), a "most ridiculous monster" (165), etc.

Anti-Semitism

There are exactly three Jews in Shakespeare's works, and all of them appear in *The Merchant of Venice.* Three Jews out of more than a thousand characters seems a paltry, if not discriminatory, ratio, but given the way two of them are treated it's perhaps a blessing. Besides, the actual number of Jews in Shakespeare's London was proportionally even tinier—about a hundred in all, as compared to a total population of around 200,000. Their number in the countryside approached to zero.

Even the Jews in London were Christian converts, at least in name. Practicing Jews were banned by law, as they had been since the early 14th century. The situation was little better elsewhere in Europe, where Jews could be found only in major commercial centers, though in some of them they were allowed to practice their religion. The exception to this generally dismal rule—as you might guess from Shakespeare's *Merchant*—was Venice, home of the original "ghettoes," where thousands of Jews had settled by the 1590s.

Before we get into what Shakespeare actually says about Jews, it may help to know that popular opinion was very much against them. Hated and feared by the vastly more numerous Christian populace, Jews figure in Renaissance literature more or less as cardboard villains—latter-day Christ-killers, diabolical schemers, and avaricious usurers. "Usury" was the tendentious term for money-lending, which Christians considered at least shameful if not downright sinful. In medieval times, lending money for interest was actually illegal (as it would remain in England until the later 16th century); and since somebody had to do it, the job devolved largely onto Jews. (Jewish financiers and capitalists were very useful, which is why they were tolerated.) Thus the terms "Jew" and "usurer" became almost inseparable in the Christian mind, even after laws against money-lending had been lifted, and when Christians as well as Jews sought ways to circumvent caps on interest rates.

Which brings us to Shakespeare's most famous Jew: Shylock the bloodthirsty moneylender, the antihero of *The Merchant of Venice.* Shylock's function, in a nutshell, is to cause trouble for Antonio, the merchant of the title; when Antonio defaults on a loan, Shylock demands what they'd agreed to: a pound of Antonio's flesh. The fashion for some time now has been to play Shylock as a tragic figure, driven to revenge by the hatred and resentment of his fellow Venetians, including and especially the saintly Antonio, who proudly abuses him. Shylock has, in fact, been held up as proof that the Bard was no anti-Semite, since the Jew is sympathetic and his Christian enemies are pious hypocrites.

And it's true that Shylock is much more interesting than the usual Jewish villain, such as the frenetic ogre Barabas in Marlowe's *The Jew of Malta.* Shakespeare gives his Jew more psychological depth, plus credible motives for his miserliness, bitterness, and hatred of Christians—they're all basically defense strategies in a hostile world. It's worth noting, though, that Shakespeare does a similar favor for the deformed and thus unloved butcher Richard III. That Shylock is no mere Christian-hating Jew, but a Christian-hating Jew with depth, makes *The Merchant of Venice* more effective than *The Jew of Malta,* but it doesn't make Shylock a hero.

In fact, Shylock is greedy, stingy, merciless, cold, and contemptuous; he hates the merchant Antonio for being a Christian and also because "He lends money gratis," which deflates Shylock's usurious rates. (Antonio would be a much less effective saint if he charged interest.) And however understandable Shylock's rage against the Christians who spit at him and kick him, who call him a "misbeliever" and a "cut-throat dog" (*Merchant* I.iii.111), we're surely not meant to applaud his murderous pursuit of a pound of Antonio's flesh.

To see Shylock as a victim is to buy his self-serving rhetoric, which nobody seems to have done for quite some time after Shakespeare's death. We can't know for sure how Shylock was originally played on the stage; but if Shylock

weren't the villain, the play would be an incoherent failure. An audience which identifies with him rather than with Antonio would be left very unsatisfied—if not angry—by the play's conclusion, in which Shylock is dispossessed, humiliated, and forced to convert to Catholicism.

After 1605, the original text of *Merchant* wouldn't be performed for another 136 years. No reason is known for the gap between 1605 and 1640; however, between 1640 and 1740, Shakespeare was hardly performed at all, except in more "sophisticated" adaptations. Among these was *The Jew of Venice*, which was frequently staged in the earlier 18th century. In this version, Shylock is reduced to a farcical villain, relieved both of his darkness and his pathos. It's unlikely these qualities were considered an essential feature of Shylock's original character. Restoration adaptations were generally made easier for an audience to swallow; but characters are more tenacious than plots, and it's probably safe to assume that Shakespeare's Shylock was viewed largely as a comic villain, not as a tragic antihero.

On the other hand, the play would be pretty hollow if Shylock were indeed the mere comic ogre of the adaptation. In Shakespeare's hands he's at least a human being who bleeds when pricked, and the more human he is the more depth, complexity, and tension there is in the play. These qualities especially appeal to modern readers and audiences, but they are also likely to seduce us into a false sense of Shakespeare's modernity. Being Shakespeare, he never wrote a simple, straightforward comedy with an uncomplicated happy ending—*The Comedy of Errors* is about as close as he got. But the complications of *Merchant* don't add up to a 20th-century attitude.

To put this all in perspective, let's look at general references to Jews in *Merchant* and other plays. Aside from praising Shylock's daughter Jessica—a "beautiful pagan" (II.iii.11) who proves herself "a gentle [gentile] and no Jew" (II.vi.51) by stealing her father's money and eloping with a Christian—Shakespeare's characters have nothing nice to say. They treat Jews as, at best, remote, strange, and generally undesirable. A favorite saying is "If I don't do such-and-such, I'm a Jew"—which is meant to mean something grotesquely improbable. Some examples:

■ Contradicted in the midst of an outrageous lie, Falstaff blusters, "You rogue, they were bound, every man of them, or I am a Jew else, an Ebrew Jew" (*1 Henry IV,* II.iv.178–79).

■ "If I do not take pity of her," Benedick muses in *Much Ado,* "I am a villain; if I do not love her, I am a Jew" (II.iii.262–63).

■ In *Two Gentlemen,* the clown Launce bids his cohort Speed to "go with me to the alehouse; if not, thou art an Hebrew, a Jew, and not worth the name of a Christian" (II.v.53–55).

■ Another clown, Launcelot Gobbo, frets that his master Shylock, being Jewish, is thus a "kind of devil" (*Merchant,* II.ii.24). In fact, he's "the very devil incarnation" (27–28). Though duty tells him to stay in Shylock's service, Launcelot is ruled by his fear and resolves to flee; "for I am a Jew if I serve the Jew any longer" (112–13).

Excepting Gobbo's "devil" remarks, these references are disrespectful but not very harmful. But Shakespeare does occasionally haul out the heavy ammunition, and it should make you think twice about his sympathies.

■ "Jewish" is sometimes synonymous with "hard-hearted." When his dog Crab shows insufficient remorse as Launce parts from his family, the clown grumbles that "A Jew would have wept to see our parting" (*Two Gentlemen,* II.iii.11–12). In *The Merchant of Venice,* Antonio rhetorically wonders "what's harder" than Shylock's "Jewish heart" (*Merchant*, IV.i.79–80).

■ *The Merchant of Venice* is of course full of anti-Semites, the saintly merchant Antonio among them. By Shylock's account, Antonio has called him a "misbeliever" and a "cutthroat dog," has spit in his beard and kicked him. Antonio doesn't deny it, and in fact promises to do so again (I.iii.111–131). Nonetheless, Shylock agrees to lend him money, which prompts Antonio to observe, "The Hebrew will turn Christian: he grows kind" (178). The fondest hope of Shylock's daughter is to marry a Venetian and "Become a Christian" (II.iii.21), and the poetic justice Shylock is served at the end of the play is forceful conversion.

■ Other terms for Shylock include "faithless Jew" (II.iv.37); "the villain Jew" (II.viii.4); "the dog Jew" (14); "harsh Jew" (IV.i.123), "inexecrable dog" (128); and "this currish Jew" (292).

■ Speaking of Christ-killers, when Falstaff writes Mistress Page a bombastic mash note, she exclaims, "What a Herod of Jewry is this!" (*Merry Wives,* II.i.20)—a reference to the "ranting villain" of traditional religious plays *(Riverside).* This bogeyman rears his head no fewer than four times in *Antony and Cleopatra.*

■ The ugliest moment of all occurs in *Macbeth.* Brewing up their double trouble, the witches toss "liver of blaspheming Jew" in the pot (IV.i.26).

Ethnic Insensitivity

A host of other nations and ethnic groups are regular butts of Shakespearean slurs and jibes. The English were by and large rather xenophobic, a condition exacerbated by their geographic insularity and their history of conflict with neighbors, particularly France and Spain. They viewed the Irish, whom they'd conquered, with almost pure contempt, though oddly enough Shakespeare leaves them alone. (The Irish situation was perhaps too sensitive.) He preferred to pick on more formidable nations, such as France.

THE TURKS

The Turks are treated with particular vitriol, partly because they were Muslims (i.e., heathens), and partly because of their long history of aggression against the Christian West. The English, like most Europeans, still hadn't gotten over the Crusades; and in the more recent past the Ottoman Empire had subjugated much of southeastern Europe and threatened other parts of Italy and the Holy Roman Empire. In Othello, the "Turk" is the bitter enemy of Venice, also functioning, in the words of Frank Kermode, as "an enemy of civility and grace, a type of cunning and disorder" (*Riverside*, 1201).

▪ Of the impertinent Phebe, Rosalind remarks, "Why, she defies me,/ Like Turk to Christian." Rosalind also gets in a racist jab in remarking on a nasty note from Phebe: "Women's gentle brain/ Could not drop forth such giant-rude invention,/ Such Ethiop words, blacker in their effect/ Than in their countenance" (*As You Like It*, IV.iii.32–36).

▪ The common phrase *turn Turk* means "go bad," as in "if the rest of my fortunes turn Turk with me" (*Hamlet*, III.ii.276).

When Beatrice shows signs of lovesickness, Margaret quips, "Well, and you be not turn'd Turk, there's no more sailing by the star" (*Much Ado*, III.iv.57–58).

■ Turks were also known for an elaborately boring prose style. "Here's a silly stately style indeed!" exclaims Pucelle upon a speech by Sir William Lucy. "The Turk, that two and fifty kingdoms hath,/ Writes not so tedious a style as this" (*1 Henry VI*, IV.vii.72–74).

■ In his first speech as King Henry V, the former Prince Hal reassures old adversaries that he will not govern from personal resentment: "This is the English, not the Turkish court,/ Not Amurath an Amurath succeeds,/ But Harry Harry" (*2 Henry IV*, V.ii.47–49). That is, he will be a moral and civilized ruler, like his father ("Harry" the Fourth), and unlike such Turkish sultans as Amurath III, who upon succeeding his father in 1574 had his brothers strangled.

■ What Hal fails to mention is that his father got the throne by deposing and executing Richard II. As the Bishop of Carlisle had predicted then, this immoral and uncivilized act would inevitably lead to bloody civil war: "The blood of English shall manure the ground,/ And future ages groan for this foul act./ Peace shall go sleep with Turks and infidels" (*Richard II*, IV.i.137–39). Carlisle's slur presumes that the Turks and infidels are neither peaceful nor deserving of peace.

■ In the witches' pot with "liver of blaspheming Jew" (page 106) are "nose of Turk and Tartar's lips" (*Macbeth*, IV.i.29). Like the Turks, the dark-skinned Tartars were viewed as hard-hearted heathens. The Duke of Venice alludes to "brassy bosoms and rough hearts of flints," namely those of "stubborn Turks, and Tartars never train'd/ To offices of tender courtesy" (*Merchant*, IV.i.31–33). Helena reprises the theme in *All's Well* with a reference to "flinty Tartar's bosom" (IV.iv.7). See also Lysander's "tawny Tartar," (page 100).

■ When Helena saves the French king's life, he promises her the choice of a husband from among France's leading bachelors. Except none of the bachelors is willing. "Do all they deny her?" asks an astonished Lafew. "And they were sons of mine, I'd have them whipt, or I would send them to th' Turk to make eunuchs of" (*AWW,* II.iii.86–88).

■ That the Turkish sultan had a harem is useful for certain metaphors. "Wine lov'd I deeply," says Edgar, playing "Poor Tom"; "and in woman out-paramour'd the Turk" (*Lear,* III.iv.90–92).

■ The profane Pistol curses Falstaff as a "Base Phrygian Turk" (*Merry Wives,* I.iii.88).

■ In a variation on the "else I'm a Jew" theme (page 105), Iago protests that he's telling the truth "or else I am a Turk" (*Othello,* II.i.114).

■ In his swan song, Othello likens himself to "a malignant and a turban'd Turk," a "circumcised dog" he once stabbed to death (*Othello,* V.ii.353–55).

THE FRENCH

Much more familiar to Shakespeare than the Turks were those perennial rivals of England, the French. Allusions to the French are much less outlandish—nothing on the order of "circumcised dog." But they're also more common and often rather contemptuous.

Shakespeare's opinion of France is perhaps reflected in how few plays he set there. *As You Like It* was the first, but it really has nothing at all to do with France, aside from the name "Jaques." The protagonists of *All's Well That Ends Well* are more assertively French, but it is not to their credit, for they are profane, conceited, and frivolous. *Love's Labor's Lost* is staged in Navarre, which borders on France, but that doesn't count, and anyway its Frenchmen are frivolous, too. The only other plays with major scenes in France are histories such as *1 Henry VI*, *King John*, and *Henry V*—but in those, France is the enemy.

▨ The French apparently didn't know the meaning of "safe sex," for they were famous in England for their socially transmitted diseases, collectively known as the "French pox" or the "malady of France." (The malady kills Doll Tearsheet in *Henry V*.) The Bard's favorite VD joke involves a pun on "French crown," which in one sense means "gold coin" but in another "bald pate"—the pox was supposed to make your hair fall out. Here's one example:

Bottom. What beard were I best to play [Pyramus] in?
Quince. Why, what you will.
Bottom. I will discharge it in either your straw-color beard, your orange-tawny beard, your purple-in-grain beard, or your French-crown-color beard, your perfit yellow.
Quince. Some of your French crowns have no hair at all; and then you will play barefac'd.

A Midsummer Night's Dream, I.ii.90–98

Shakespeare never tires of this joke; the pun appears six more times in a variety of plays.

▪ In a different but equally charming way, King Henry puns on French coins in *Henry V.* Referring to the forthcoming English-French showdown, in which the former are vastly outnumbered, Henry admits that "the French may lay twenty French crowns to one they will beat us, for they bear them on their shoulders" (i.e., they have twenty "crowns" or heads to each English one). "But it is no English treason," says Henry, "to cut French crowns, and to-morrow the King himself will be a clipper" (IV.i.225–29). In case that flew by you, what the king is saying is that it's perfectly fine for Englishmen to cut off French heads. He's looking forward to it himself.

▪ In a verbal skirmish with the bawdy Lucio, a nameless Viennese gentleman puns on the words *piled* ("napped") and *pilled* ("bald"), both abbreviated as *pil'd:*

> thou art good velvet; thou'rt a three-pil'd piece, I warrant thee. I had as lief be a list [strip] of an English kersey [plain fabric] as be pil'd, as thou art pil'd, for a French velvet.
>
> *Measure for Measure,* I.ii.31–34

Decoded, the gentleman's point is that he'd rather be a dull but healthy Englishman than a fashionable but "pilled" Frenchman, balding from the French pox. The shame about some of these French jokes is that by the time one is done explaining them, the timing has been ruined and they're no longer very funny.

▪ The French are regularly mocked for their social affectations, judged absurd by Shakespeare's (slightly) less flamboyant countrymen. Take the "French brawl"—not a fight, but a rather peculiar form of performance art. According to Moth, to do the French brawl is to

> jig off a tune at the tongue's end, canary to it with your feet, humor it with turning up your eyelids, sigh a note and sing a note, sometime through the throat, as if you swallow'd love with singing love, sometime through the nose, as if you snuff'd up love by smelling love; with your hat penthouse-like o'er the shop of your eyes; with your arms cross'd on your thin-bellied doublet like a rabbit on a spit; or your hands in your pocket like a man after the old painting; and keep not too long in one tune, but a snip and away.

Love's Labor's Lost, III.i.11–22

On the other hand, one could see such behavior provoking the other kind of brawl, especially since the French were apparently also known to be quarrelsome.

▧ There's more where thin-bellied doublets (tight waistjackets) came from. There are, for example, the Constable's "French hose" (big breeches) and "straight strossers" (tight underpants) in *Henry V* (III.vii.53–54). These hose are also sported by the affected English suitor Falconbridge in *Merchant,* who "bought his doublet in Italy, his round hose in France, his bonnet in Germany, and his behavior every where" (I.ii.74–76).

▧ "Because I cannot flatter and look fair," grumbles the trickster Richard, "Smile in men's faces, smooth, deceive, and cog,/ Duck with French nods and apish courtesy,/ I must be held a rancorous enemy" (*Richard III,* I.iii.47–50). Clearly, "French nods" are insincerely fawning gestures, all the worse for being imported from the supersubtle French court, presumably a bastion of hypocrisy and "cogging" (deceit). Richard, however, deceives more by claiming not to deceive than he would have with French nods.

■ More elaborate is the catalogue of "courtesies" (courtly gestures) ascribed to the Frenchman Boyet in *Love's Labor's Lost:*

> This gallant pins the wenches on his sleeve;
> Had he been Adam, he had tempted Eve.
> 'A can carve too, and lisp; why, this is he
> That kiss'd his hand away in courtesy;
> This is the ape of form, monsieur the nice,
> That when he plays at tables chides the dice
> In honorable terms; nay, he can sing
> A mean [tenor] most meanly, and in hushering
> Mend him who can. The ladies call him sweet;
> The stairs as he treads on them kiss his feet.
> This is the flow'r that smiles on every one,
> To show his teeth as white as whale's bone;
> And consciences that will not die in debt
> Pay him the due of honey-tongued Boyet.

> V.ii.321–34

The most galling item is probably the whalebone-white teeth, given the state of your average Englishman's gums.

■ Earlier in *Love's Labor's Lost,* the Spaniard Don Armado refers to "a new-devis'd cur'sy" of "any French courtier" (I.ii.62–63), another allusion to the French talent for concocting ("devising") new-fangled courtly gestures. The Arden edition glosses Armado's "new-devised courtesy" as a "bow or complimentary acknowledgment after any of the new French fashions."

■ In *Henry VIII*, the Lord Chamberlain exchanges a few choice remarks with Sir Thomas Lovell on the theme of French fashions. English gallants who cross the Channel learn only to "fill the court with quarrels, talk, and tailors," says Lovell (I.iii.20). "I would pray our monsieurs," the Lord Chamberlain replies, "To think an English courtier may be wise/ And never see the Louvre" (21–23). Lovell goes on to abuse a whole list of French fashions, such as "tennis and tall stockings," "blist'red breaches," and so forth. "The sly whoresons," he concludes, "Have got a speeding trick to lay down ladies./ A French song and a fiddle has no fellow" (39–41).

■ The insults flow pretty freely in *1 Henry VI*, which blatantly pandered to English chauvinism. (It was a huge hit.) The hero Talbot, for instance, puns hilariously on the Christian name of Joan of Arc ("Pucelle") and the English title for the French dauphin ("Dolphin"):

> Pucelle or puzzel, Dolphin or dogfish,
> Your hearts I'll stamp out with my horse's heels,
> And make a quagmire of your mingled brains.

> I.iv.107–9

A puzzel is a slut, and a dogfish a shark. Two lines later Talbot spits fire at "dastard Frenchmen" (111).

■ When the wavering Duke of Burgundy abandons his alliance with the English to return to the side of his French countrymen, Pucelle (a French heroine!) snidely remarks, "Done like a Frenchman—turn and turn again!" (*1 Henry VI*, III.iii.85). At the French palace two scenes later, King Henry cautions his lords to "remember where we

RACIST, ANTI-SEMITE, XENOPHOBE? ▦ 115

are—/ In France, amongst a fickle, wavering nation" (IV.i.137–38).

■ Astonishingly, Shakespeare manages to match the jingoism of *1 Henry VI* in his later history *King John,* in which France and the French are cursed and derided in innumerable ways. For example, when King Philip, like Burgundy in the earlier play, abandons a pact with the English, Elinor cries, "O foul revolt of French inconstancy!" (*John,* III.i.322). John himself mocks the "coward hand of France" (II.i.158), though he will later go on to shake it, much to the dismay of all the sensible characters in the play.

■ To spur on his troops against the Breton supporters of his rival Richmond, Richard III bellows these rousing lines:

> Remember whom you are to cope withal:
> A sort of vagabonds, rascals, and runaways,
> A scum of Britains [Bretons] and base lackey peasants,
> Whom their o'ercloyed country vomits forth
> To desperate adventures and assur'd destruction....
> Let's whip these stragglers o'er the seas again;
> Lash hence these overweening rags of France....
> If we be conquered, let men conquer us,
> And not these bastard Britains....
>
> *Richard III,* V.iii.315–33

The Breton/Britain confusion sort of spoils the effect, but we're not supposed to be rooting for Richard, anyway.

■ "Masters, you are all welcome," Hamlet cries to a group of traveling players. "We'll e'en to 't like French falc'ners—fly at any thing we see; we'll have a speech straight" (*Hamlet,*

II.ii.429–31). Hamlet slights the French ability to handle a bird, certainly unjustly but probably in line with the chauvinistic English notion.

■ The rascal Parolles urges the heroine Helena to be "off with" her virginity "while 'tis vendible" (that is, while she's young and attractive). For

> your virginity, your old virginity, is like one of our French wither'd pears, it looks ill, it eats drily, marry, 'tis a wither'd pear; it was formerly better, marry, yet 'tis a wither'd pear.

All's Well, I.i.160–63

Whether French pears more closely resembled the female privates than any other pears is somewhat doubtful; Parolles may specify "French" in a merely generic way—the play is, after all, largely set in France. On the other hand, there's no doubt the "French wither'd pears" sounds funny, and that it also makes the speech somehow more dirty.

■ "France is a dog-hole," explains the Frenchman Parolles (*All's Well,* II.ii.274); or, on second thought, "France is a stable" (284).

■ And much, much more!

THE ITALIANS

In contrast to the French, the Italians come out of Shakespeare practically unscathed—the Vatican excepted. The principal or partial setting of roughly a dozen plays, Italy is generally an exotic and romantic backdrop for passionate dramas (whose plots are mostly borrowed from Italian literature)—*The Merchant of Venice, Romeo and Juliet, Othello,* and so forth. Some characters are as bad as the French, but rarely are they bad *because* they're Italian.

■ An exception to this rule is the malicious trickster Iachimo in *Cymbeline,* the one play in which Italy (Rome) is at war with Britain. Iachimo, who bears an interesting resemblance to Iago, is a "Slight thing of Italy" (V.iv.64) and an "Italian fiend" (V.v.210), at once frivolous and diabolical. Both the Venetian Iago and the Florentine Iachimo are partly inspired by that most infamous of Renaissance Italians, Niccolò Machiavelli. The English even coined the term *Machiavel* for amoral manipulators, crafty politicians, and nihilists in general. "Am I politic?" asks the Host in *The Merry Wives of Windsor;* "Am I subtle? Am I a Machiavel?" (*Wives,* III.i.101). Ironically, the greatest—that is, the worst—of Shakespeare's Machiavels is an Englishman: King Richard III (see *3 Henry VI,* III.ii.193).

■ Italians were also famed as Europe's premier druggists, with a particular mastery of such "potions" and "mortal drugs" (poisons) as Romeo and Friar Lawrence acquire in *Romeo and Juliet.* In *Cymbeline,* again, Imogen curses "drug-damn'd Italy" (III.iv.15), an even apter phrase given that Iachimo has poisoned her husband Posthumus's heart against her. This prompts Posthumus's servant Pisanio to marvel, in soliloquy,

> O master, what a strange infection
> Is fall'n into thy ear! What false Italian
> (As poisonous tongu'd as handed) hath prevail'd
> On thy too ready hearing?

> *Cymbeline,* III.ii.3–6

Once again, however, the Italians have good company. Earlier in the play, the wicked (British) Queen buys from her (British) physician some "poisonous compounds" which he claims are "the movers of a languishing death" (I.v.8–9).

■ There's also much talk in the play about the bewitching "shes of Italy" (*Cymbeline*, I.iii.29), whose charms are as unnatural as foreign potions. Imogen worries that Posthumus has been snared by "Some jay of Italy/ (Whose mother was her painting)" (III.iv.49–50)—that is, by a painted bird ("jay") who is the "creature of her cosmetics" *(Riverside)*.

■ The French were no less susceptible than the English to Italian charms, artificial or natural. "Those girls of Italy, take heed of them," warns the king in *All's Well*. "They say our French lack the language to deny/ If they demand" (II.i.19–21).

■ Elsewhere, we hear "Report of fashions in proud Italy,/ Whose manners still our tardy, apish nation/ Limps after in base imitation" (*Richard II*, II.i.21–23). The English, whose native "fashions" consisted of such stuff as plain kersey wool, sought their pizzazz in Italy, whose styles were considered somewhat less ridiculous than the French.

THE SPANISH

The one true Spaniard in Shakespeare is Don Armado, a buffoonish hanger-on in *Love's Labor's Lost*. His name mockingly alludes to the Spanish Armada, whose threats were repelled by the English navy in 1588, roughly seven years before the play was written.

The bombastic Armado is a bit fruitier and more exotic

than your average Frenchman but much in the same mold. He fancies himself a "refined traveller," according to the King of Navarre, who also notes that he's a "man in all the world's new fashion planted" and who "hath a mint of phrases in his brain" (*LLL,* I.i.163–65). That is, he's a trendy fashion-monger who spouts all the latest catch-phrases, many of them culled from the jargon of fencing. Armado is even more self-important than the Frenchman Boyet, who calls him a "phantasime" (fantasist) and a "Monarcho" (conceited braggart) (IV.i.99).

Spanish bombast becomes proverbial in the mouth of pro-fane Pistol: "When Pistol lies, do this [*makes obscene gesture*], and fig me like/ The bragging Spaniard" (*2 Henry IV,* V.iii.118–19). In his next play, he swears at Fluellen in a similar vein: "The fig of Spain!" (*Henry V,* III.vi.59). "Fig" is one of Pistol's regular obscenities—see page 188.

THE GREEKS

Most of the abuse directed at Greeks is delivered by Trojans in *Troilus and Cressida.* This is to be expected and can be safely discounted, so I will pass it over, except for one interesting case.

"I swear to you," Pandarus lies, "I think Helen loves him [Troilus] better than Paris." "Then she's a merry Greek indeed," Cressida puns (*Troilus,* I.ii.107–9). "Merry Greek" meant "he-donist" or "self-indulger," a notion perhaps derived from an old Roman stereotype of Greeks as loose-living Epicureans.

Cressida will use the phrase again later, after learning that she's been traded to the enemy: "A woeful Cressid 'mongst the merry Greeks!" she predicts (IV.iv.56). Given that she's saying good-bye to her grieving lover Troilus, the joke is a bit inap-propriate, but that seems lost on him. In fact, Cressida will have a merry, not woeful, time in the Greek camp, especially with the dashing Diomed.

▪ Merriness is just a few notches short of folly. And thus, per-haps, impatient Sebastian's plea to Feste, who's pestering him: "I prithee, foolish Greek, depart from me" (*Twelfth Night,* IV.i.18).

▪ About the most serious charge against the Greeks is that their language is unintelligible. Thus "Greek" may some-times mean "gobbledygook" and sometimes deliberately confusing cant, such as the banter of a con man. "Duc-dame, ducdame, ducdame!" chants the sourpuss Jaques; "What's that 'ducdame'?" asks puzzled Amiens; "'Tis a Greek invocation," Jaques replies, "to call fools into a circle" (*As You Like It,* II.v.54–59). When Cassius asks Casca what Cicero said, the stymied Casca admits, "for mine own part, it was Greek to me" (*Caesar,* I.iii.283).

THE DUTCH

As England's most active trading partners, the Dutch were the most neighborly of all neighbors—especially since they were fellow Protestants, unlike the Irish, French, Italians, Por-tuguese, and Spanish. Nonetheless, they come in for their share of negative stereotyping. And it has mostly to do with food and drink.

▪ Take, for instance, Iago's epithet "swag-bellied Hollander" (*Othello,* II.iii.78), which means "beer-bellied Dutchman." The Dutch were considered terrible drunkards and were ac-cused by some of spreading their sinful ways to England. In fact the point of Iago's speech is that the English have be-come more formidable tipplers even than the Dutch: "Why, he [an Englishman] drinks you, with facility, your Dane dead drunk; he sweats not to overthrow your Almain [German]; he gives your Hollander a vomit ere the next pottle [tankard] can be fill'd" (82–85).

▪ And then there's Dutch food. Falstaff details his frightful experience of being buried in a laundry basket, practically suffocating, and sweating profusely, "more than half stew'd in grease, like a Dutch dish" (*Wives,* III.v.118–19). Yum.

▪ Finally, there's Prince Hal's questionable joke in *2 Henry IV,* where he scolds Poins for absenting the tennis courts "because the rest of thy low countries have made a shift to eat up thy holland" (II.ii.21–22). On one level he's saying that Poins has no outfit to play in, as his "low" entertainments have forced him to trade ("shift") his linens ("holland") for cash. (Holland was England's principal source of finished fabrics.) But Hal seems to mean something more by "low countries" and "holland"—most likely Poins's own nether regions (front and back) and their business. A similar pun is found in *The Comedy of Errors,* where Dromio of Syracuse recoils in horror from a fat wench's "Netherlands": "O, sir," he tells his master, "I did not look so low" (III.ii.138–39).

THE DANES

Iago groups the Danes with the Germans and Dutch as notorious drunks (see above), an assessment confirmed by Prince Hamlet of Denmark himself. Observing that King Claudius is up late taking his "rouse" (i.e., carousing), keeping "wassail" (carousing), and draining down "his draughts of Rhenish" (carousing), Hamlet remarks that such behavior is a Danish custom, but "a custom/ More honor'd in the breach than the observance" (*Hamlet,* I.iv.8–16)—that is, a practice more honorable to abstain from than to indulge.

The Prince serves up a number of other opinions on his homeland, for example: "Denmark's a prison" (II.ii.243), and "there are many confines, wards, and dungeons, Denmark being one o' th' worst" (245–47). In the famous words of Marcellus, "Something is rotten in the state of Denmark" (I.iv.90).

THE GERMANS

The Germans (like their hard-drinking fellows the Dutch and the Danes) were Protestants. Thus they were friends, and aside from the following nasty swipes, Shakespeare treats them gently.

▦ In *The Merchant of Venice,* Nerissa asks Portia what she thinks of her German suitor. "Very vildly [vilely] in the morning," replies Portia, "when he is sober, and most vildly in the afternoon, when he is drunk" (I.ii.86–87). Furthermore, "When he is best, he is little worse than a man, and when he is worst, he is little better than a beast" (88–89). In conclusion, "I will do any thing, Nerissa, ere I will be married to a sponge" (98–99).

▦ Germans were celebrated as clockmakers, but Berowne doesn't think much of their workmanship. He jokes that a wife is like "a German clock,/ Still a-repairing, ever out of frame" (*LLL,* III.i.190–91)—i.e., always out of order and ever in need of repair.

▦ In his long and very boring colloquy with King Henry on obscure international pacts, the Archbishop of Canterbury recalls that Charles the Great, "holding in disdain the German women/ For some dishonest manners of their life," barred them from inheriting land (*Henry V,* I.ii.48–51). In other words, he thought they were all sluts.

Dishes and Devils

There are many remarkable female characters in Shakespeare. There are, for example, the learned and long-suffering Portia *(Merchant);* the witty and forceful Kate *(Shrew)* and Beatrice *(Much Ado);* that spicy brunette Hermia *(Dream)* and the poetic pubescent Juliet *(Romeo);* brave and resourceful disguisers such as Julia *(Two Gentlemen),* Rosalind *(As You Like It),* and Viola *(Twelfth Night);* fiery Cleopatra *(Antony);* and the spirited but patiently virtuous types of the later plays— Helena *(All's Well),* Isabella *(Measure),* Desdemona *(Othello),* Cordelia *(Lear),* Imogen *(Cymbeline),* Marina *(Pericles),* Hermione *(Winter's Tale),* and Miranda *(Tempest).*

This catalogue of female power is certainly impressive, and no one else in Shakespeare's day came close to matching it. It's also a prima facie case for the Bard's liberated viewpoint: many of these women know what they want, they deserve it, and they're not afraid to demand it. Sometimes (as in *As You Like It, Twelfth Night,* and *All's Well*), they even control large portions of the plot until they get it.

But a few points make us hesitate. For example: what they "want" usually turns out to be marriage, often to dominating and very unliberated men. That is, they get to be unconventional for four acts or so before being reabsorbed into a conventional, male world that reflects (in idealized form) the sad Elizabethan reality to which these women are temporary exceptions. The world of Shakespeare's comedies and romances—where practically all these ladies appear—is a realm of fantasy, a "holiday" from the tedious and oppressing everyday world of forced marriages and male domination.

If for this reason the comedies fail to please today's feminists, they also pose problems for today's moralists. The latter can't very well proclaim the uplifting traditional virtues of plays that defied both tradition and the family. In the words of Andrew Gurr, "Shakespeare's heroines were an alarming novelty." They spurned the authority and the wishes of their parents (particularly their fathers) to pursue their own desires; and one can only imagine the horror with which London citizens greeted the spectacle of Juliet's defiance, and the sympathy with which they received the ravings of her furious father Capulet.

In the end, Shakespeare had his cake and ate it too. His assertive and sometimes bawdy females must have delighted the women in his audience, but everybody knew they were fantasies, and male fantasies at that. (Or, in the cases of Kate and Beatrice, male nightmares—until they're tamed.) No Elizabethan young lady is known to have survived a shipwreck in order to woo a duke while dressed as a boy, as Viola does in *Twelfth Night*.

And that's the good news. Shakespeare's remaining female characters—all played on stage by boys (see page 179)—are by and large either set decorations,  shrews, dimbulbs, prostitutes, or savages. The Bard shows little enthusiasm for such proper types as Luciana *(Errors)*, Bianca *(Shrew)*, or Hero *(Much Ado)*, who look nice on stage but are all forgettable. Hamlet's Ophelia isn't much better until she goes crazy, while Hamlet's mother is weak and morally bankrupt. Quickly's dumb; Cressida's loose; Doll Tearsheet and Bianca are whores; and Regan, Goneril, and Lady Macbeth are monsters.

■ ■ ■

To be fair, most of the bad females are fantasies too, so Shakespeare scores about even. "A woman is a dish for the gods, if the devil dress her not" (*Antony*, V.ii.274)—she's a heavenly sex object or a hell-bent shrew, but in either case she's nowhere on earth. For every heroine who's bold, free, and in control of her destiny, there's a Dark Lady whose goal is to humiliate and cheat on men. And many of the free spirits end up back where they belong, safely married and at home. By act V it's a man's world again, and along the way we sometimes meet with oppressive opinions on the fairer sex. Listen to Petruchio gloat while he humiliates his "sweet wench" and new wife, Kate:

> Carouse full measure to her maidenhead,
> Be mad and merry, or go hang yourselves;
> But for my bonny Kate, she must with me.
> Nay, look not big, nor stamp, nor stare, nor fret,
> I will be master of what is mine own.
> She is my goods, my chattels, she is my house,
> My household stuff, my field, my barn,
> My horse, my ox, my ass, my any thing.

> *The Taming of the Shrew*, III.ii.225–32

Kate herself makes the same point later at greater length, after she's tamed and fit for a comic ending:

> Thy husband is thy lord, thy life, thy keeper,
> Thy head, thy sovereign; one that cares for thee,
> And for thy maintenance; commits his body
> To painful labor, both by sea and land;
> To watch the night in storms, the day in cold,
> Whilst thou li'st warm at home, secure and safe;
> And craves no other tribute at thy hands

> But love, fair looks, and true obedience—
> Too little payment for so great a debt.
> Such duty as the subject owes the prince,
> Even such a woman oweth to her husband;
> And when she is froward, peevish, sullen, sour,
> And not obedient to his honest will,
> What is she but a foul contending rebel,
> And graceless traitor to her loving lord?
> I am asham'd that women are so simple
> To offer war where they should kneel for peace,
> Or seek for rule, supremacy, and sway,
> When they are bound to serve, love, and obey.
>
> *Shrew,* V.ii.146–64

In short, "shut up and obey," a point which gains force in the mouth of a reformed shrew. "Why, there's a wench!" Petruchio cries. "Come on, and kiss me, Kate" (179–80). Shakespeare's men love submissive women.

■   ■   ■

Kate's not the only one to sit down for her sex. Though proud of her "man's mind," Portia is excellent despite her feminine weaknesses: "How hard it is for women to keep counsel!" she sighs (*Caesar,* II.iv.9). She clarifies this later: "Ay me, how week a thing/ The heart of woman is!" (39–40). "Unsex me here!" cries Lady Macbeth, knowing she strives beyond the deeds of women (*Macbeth,* I.v.41).

Though she may be kidding, Rosalind still echoes the stereotype of female loquacity: "Do you not know I am a woman? When I think, I must speak" (*AYL,* III.ii.249–50). Lucetta is more serious when she explains her liking for Proteus this way: "I have no other reason but a woman's reason:/ I think him so, because I think him so" (*TGV,* I.ii.23–24).

▪ ▪ ▪

As they make some manly jokes, celebrating King Henry's conquest of Katherine, Burgundy tells the king that "maids, well summer'd and warm kept, are like flies at Bartholomew-tide"—late August—"blind, though they have their eyes, and then they will endure handling, which before would not abide looking on" (*Henry V,* V.ii.307–11). That is, if young ladies are well kept in the summer, they're less apt to object to fondling in the fall.

Women are often depicted as easy conquests in Shakespeare. He even wrote a whole play about it, *Troilus and Cressida.* As we'll see later, this is on the one hand great for men, and on the other absolutely maddening (page 134). No suitor need infer from a lady's coolness that she wants him to leave her alone. "She is a woman, therefore may be woo'd," opines lustful Demetrius of the already married Lavinia; "She is a woman, therefore may be won" (*Titus,* II.i.82–83). And as the (married) Suffolk admires a young French beauty, he considers that "She's beautiful; and therefore to be wooed:/ She is a woman; therefore to be won" (*1 Henry VI,* V.iii.78–79).

Women can always be persuaded, so pay no mind to anything they say. "Have you not heard it said full oft,/ A woman's nay doth stand for naught?" (*Passionate Pilgrim,* xviii.41–42). Julia admits of her sex that "maids, in modesty, say 'no' to that/ Which they would have the profferer construe as 'ay.'" (*TGV,* I.ii.55–56). In short, no means yes.

Easy conquests, however, are short-lived. As Cressida rightly remarks, "Men prize the thing ungain'd more than it is" (*Troilus,* I.ii.289). "For women," explains Orsino, "are as roses, whose fair flow'r/ Being once display'd, doth fall that very hour" (*TwN,* II.iv.38–39). So the younger and fresher you get them, the better.

▪ ▪ ▪

Despite all Shakespeare's strong women, as a sex they are rarely credited with much strength or resolve. Going from the particular of his mother to the general, Hamlet deduces that "Frailty, thy name is woman!" (*Hamlet,* I.ii.146). More kindly, Rosalind quotes the Bible's epithet, "weaker vessel" (*AYL,* II.iv.6), which is amplified by Quickly: "you are the weaker vessel, as they say, the emptier vessel" (*2 Henry IV,* II.iv.60–61).

"Women are soft, mild, pitiful, and flexible," declares the Duke of York, attempting to school the shrewish Queen Margaret (*3 Henry VI,* I.iv.141). They need steady rule and guidance, for as Friar Lawrence says, "Women may fall, when there's no strength in men" (*Romeo,* II.iii.80).

■ ■ ■

Besides being weak, women are also congenitally vain. If they ever get the idea men find them attractive, they will never let anyone forget it—for their attractiveness becomes their power. "If ladies be but young and fair,/ They have the gift to know it" (*AYL,* II.vii.37–38). Not only do they know it, they practice it: "For there was never yet fair woman," observes Lear's fool, "but she made mouths in a glass [mirror]" (*Lear,* III.ii.35–36).

But men should really know better than to fall for a pretty face. For beauty does not always come naturally, and in fact the more ladies make a show of their attractions, the more suspicious one should be. "There is never a fair woman has a true face," Enobarbus warns (*Antony,* II.vi.99–101). That is, beauty is largely cosmetic, artificial; and if it's artificial, it is "false." "I have heard of your paintings [makeup], well enough," remarks Hamlet.

"God hath given you one face, and you make yourselves another" (*Hamlet*, III.i.142–44).

On the other hand, even Nature is capable of false shows, and "with a beauteous wall/ Doth oft close in pollution" (*Twelfth Night*, I.ii.48–49). But women are still the masters of clothing pollution in beauty, as Posthumus thinks he's discovered when presented with evidence that his fair wife has been false:

> Let there be no honor
> Where there is beauty; truth, where semblance; love,
> Where there's another man. The vows of women
> Of no more bondage be to where they are made
> Than they are to their virtues, which is nothing.
> O, above measure false!
>
> *Cymbeline*, II.iv.108–13

Posthumus, however, is deceived in believing himself deceived, and his ranting against women's falsehood is an explosion of male insecurity and misogyny. Which is a subject for another chapter.

Family Values Watch

▪

Given such ideas about women, you won't be surprised to hear that marriage also comes in for a beating. If you thought the Bard was just stuffed full of happy thoughts on wedded bliss, you were wrong. Of course, most of the comedies do end in weddings, which are warmly greeted by all involved. But the whole point is that they *end* in weddings.

As for functional two-parent families, you have to use a microscope to find them. There are the Montagues and the Capulets in *Romeo and Juliet,* though "functional" isn't the word; and I doubt anyone would recommend the family in *The Winter's Tale.* Elsewhere, an alarming number of parents are separated, absent, missing, or dead. Does anyone know (or care) what happened to all the wives and mothers in *Much Ado?* Or in practically any other comedy you can name? Single fathers are the norm, not the exception; and while there were literary and practical reasons for this, it still sets a terrible example. I need only mention Lear.

So happy, healthy families are few; still, you say, marriage is the great aspiration of comedy. It's greeted with joy and applause, wonder and delight. It's true that marriage in the comedies is a triumph—but a triumph over family, over reason, and over history. When it's not the bride and groom who have to be dragged to the altar, it's their parents, whose authority and wisdom are mocked. Shakespeare's lovers, furthermore, only make good sense when they're not in love; otherwise they forget their own very sensible and convincing objections to marriage. Which is even more of a feat when there's so little evidence for the comic theory of eternal love—which turns out, in fact, to be a ruse.

▪ ▪ ▪

This is trademark Shakespeare, in whom hope is always balanced by realism, ideals always qualified by experience. And as no love sonnet goes unridiculed in his plays, no marriage escapes a hazing. *Love's Labor's Lost* is one long satire on the marital aspirations of its four foolish heroes—and the punchline is that they don't get married. (Another comedy with frustrated weddings is *The Merry Wives of Windsor*, in which two men end up eloping with boys.)

A frequent theme of such ridicule is the sad reality of actual marriage, as opposed to the poetic fancies of lovers. The problem here seems to be wives. They're adorable when you marry them, and curses thereafter. Take it from someone who knows—converted Kate in *The Taming of the Shrew*. Being cured of her wild independent notions, she now sees clearly the evils other women practice. Too often, rather than gratify her husband, a wife is "froward, peevish, sullen, sour,/ And not obedient to his honest will" (*Shrew*, V.ii.157–58). Such a wife is a "foul contending rebel," a "graceless traitor to her loving lord," hungry for power, a "froward and unable" worm (159–60, 169).

Iago, who fancies himself a harried husband, paints an equally horrid picture in *Othello*. While submissive and demure in public, wives are "Bells in your parlors" (constantly ringing) and "wild-cats in your kitchens"; "Saints in your injuries" (never to blame) but "devils being offended" (furies when crossed); "Players in your huswifery" (useless at home), and "huswives in your beds" (wanton lovers or "hussies") (*Othello,* II.i.110–12).

This impressive summary of a shrew is matched by some living examples on the stage. The first is Adriana in *The Comedy of Errors,* whose nagging and scolding actually seem warranted, but who nonetheless ends up getting lectured by an abbess: "The venom clamors of a jealous woman/ Poisons more deadly than a mad dog's tooth" (*Errors,* V.i.69–70). There's the Shrew Kate herself, of course, and there are all sorts of sour, sharp-tongued females in the *Henry VI–Richard III* cycle.

Then there's Beatrice in *Much Ado.* As she rails against men and marriage, Benedick quips, "God keep your ladyship still in that mind, so some gentleman or other shall scape a predestinate scratch'd face" (*Much Ado,* I.i.133–35). "By my troth, niece," advises her patronizing uncle, "thou wilt never get thee a husband, if thou be so shrewd of thy tongue"; to which her father replies, "In faith, she's too curst" ("sharp-tongued," II.i.18–20). You're apparently supposed to wait till *after* the wedding to be curst.

Thus the blunt assessment of the rascal Parolles: "A young man that's married is a man that's marred" (*AWW,* II.iii.298). In *The Merchant of Venice,* Nerissa quotes the fateful equation, "Hanging and wiving goes by destiny" (II.ix.82–83), which is improved on by Feste: "Many a good hanging prevents a bad marriage" (*TwN,* I.v.19–20). The ordeal of marriage is apparently so onerous that Friar Lawrence can rhyme, "She's not well married that lives married long,/ But she's best married that dies married young" (*Romeo,* IV.v.77–78).

▪ ▪ ▪

So why do men even bother? Stupidity has something to do with it. "Fools are as like husbands as pilchers are to herrings," Feste quips—"the husband's the bigger" (*TwN,* III.i.34–35). But men also have their reasons. One is money—Kate's big attraction in *Shrew.* Another is power—the true aim of seducers like Richard III and Henry V. But the main reason seems to be lust.

"My poor body, madam, requires it," the Clown explains in *All's Well.* "I am driven on by the flesh, and he must needs go that the devil drives" (I.iii.28–30). Rosalind tells a similar story:

> For your brother and my sister no sooner met but they look'd; no sooner look'd but they lov'd; no sooner lov'd but they sigh'd; no sooner sigh'd but they ask'd one another the reason; no sooner knew the reason but they sought the remedy: and in these degrees have they made a pair of stairs to marriage, which they will climb incontinent, or else be incontinent before marriage.

> *As You Like It,* V.ii.32–39

Incontinence gets Claudio in deep trouble in *Measure for Measure:* for jumping the gun, he's condemned to die. The usual punishment wasn't so dire—it was just forced marriage. But that is presumably the fate one was hoping to avoid.

▓ ▓ ▓

"I say we will have no moe marriage," rants Hamlet, who's sickened by the very idea (*Hamlet,* III.i.147). But Shakespeare gives us plenty moe marriage, often as an excuse for exploring one of his favorite themes, rampant female sexuality. Or rather, rampant male fantasies about female sexuality. It's apparently out of control. And the result is the subject of our next chapter.

Horny Shakespeare

For I the ballad will repeat,
    Which men full true shall find:
Your marriage comes by destiny,
    Your cuckoo sings by kind.

All's Well, I.iii.60–63

As we've seen (page 128), Shakespeare seems to have a problem with makeup. This is ironic, given his trade, but he's only echoing a common prejudice; many in his day regarded "face-painting" as a kind of lie. A woman who can change her face is dangerous—for who knows what else she's hiding?

This question stumps most of Shakespeare's men. Rather than leap to the obvious answer ("Probably nothing important"), they get lost in all sorts of psychological tangles. This results from two factors: (a) they are inherently and powerfully jealous; and (b) they don't trust women at all. The commonplace view is marvelously captured in *The Passionate Pilgrim,* a collection of poems partly by Shakespeare:

The wiles and guiles that women work,
Dissembled with an outward show,
The tricks and toys that in them lurk,
The cock that treads them shall not know.

xviii.37–40

The "cock" in this case is the husband, proverbial victim of his cheating hen.

Even if Shakespeare didn't write those lines, there are plenty just as bad in the plays. "In Venice," clucks Iago, "they do let God see the pranks [hanky-panky]/ They dare not show their husbands." Wives don't have enough conscience to resist, but only enough to "keep't unknown" (*Othello,* III.iii.202–4). "O curse of marriage!" Othello explodes, "That we can call these delicate creatures ours,/ And not their appetites" (268–70). "Should all despair/ That have revolted wives," observes Leontes, "the tenth of mankind/ Would hang themselves" (*Winter's Tale,* I.ii.198–200). Others put the figure higher.

The grand passions of Othello and Leontes are only part of the story in Shakespeare. They comprise what you might call the "tragic view" of female adultery—or alleged female adultery. In this scheme of things, a man deceived is a man whose beliefs are destroyed, whose reputation is shattered, and whose progeny is now in doubt. He's been stripped of his very

manhood, defiled and degraded. Thus, in Othello's immortal words, "A horned man's a monster and a beast" (*Othello*, IV.i.62). This leaves him two choices: to take revenge, or to psychologically disintegrate. Othello chooses revenge—first threatening to chop his wife to pieces, then to poison her, and finally (at Iago's suggestion) to strangle her.

The tragic view isn't confined to tragedy—*The Winter's Tale* is a tragicomedy, and the same view is taken for granted in *Much Ado about Nothing,* a comedy. The more common "comic" view, however, is not the victim's but the spectator's. Comic observers heap their mirth on humiliated men, who are viewed as foolish and impotent. Neither surprised nor shocked by the news, they merely laugh at the victim, hurling the epithet "cuckold." If he becomes dangerous they stop, but if he seems not to mind then he's a "wittol," or contented cuckold.

■ ■ ■

The term *cuckold* seems to stem from the Old French for "cuckoo," a bird known to lay eggs in others' nests. But if so the term is better suited to the adulteress than to the adulteree. More confusing is the fancy that a cuckold grows invisible horns as a mark of his wife's infidelities. It's true that *horn* could be slang for "erect penis" (thus the term *horny*), but surely the point is that the cuckold isn't "horny" enough.*

Social humiliation, or the fear of it, sometimes adds a lunatic edge to the cuckold's jealousy and rage, leading to a state called "horn madness." The pathetic Master Ford, in *The Merry Wives of Windsor,* is the purest comic victim of horn madness, and he barely crawls out from under his shame by

---

* *In lieu of a better explanation, the* OED *(sv "cuckold") speculates that the cuckold's horns refer to the "practice formerly prevalent of planting or engrafting the spurs of a castrated cock on the root of the excised comb, where they grew and became horns, sometimes several inches long."*

the end of act V. The most obvious tragic victim is Othello, who doesn't realize his plot is supposed to be comedy, and who murders his blameless wife before killing himself. *The Winter's Tale* replays *Othello,* except that the horn-mad Leontes is saved from his own intended crimes. *Cymbeline* also reprises the plot of *Othello* (the most popular tragedy of the 17th century), as Posthumus is driven horn-mad by the Iago-like schemer Iachimo. In *Much Ado,* Claudio is nearly as rabid, and, like Posthumus and Leontes, he also nearly kills an innocent woman.

In short, every horn-mad man turns out to be a fool. This only goes to prove that the Bard holds something like the comic view, namely that jealousy is folly. Not that wives don't stray, but there's not much husbands can do; and if they worry about it too much they go mad. Shakespeare, in fact, doesn't seem to think adultery is such a big deal.

Horn madness is exclusively a male disease, but that doesn't mean females don't get jealous. Cleopatra is suspicious in *Antony and Cleopatra,* but on the other hand Antony *is* married. Emilia, in *The Comedy of Errors,* is jealous with more justice, for her husband Antipholus is a cheating cad. So is Bertram in *All's Well That Ends Well,* though his wife Helena is a saint. While these men aren't exactly admirable, their shenanigans are more or less indulged, and they escape with slaps on the wrist. Desdemona ends up dead.

■ ■ ■

One of Leontes' obsessions in *The Winter's Tale* is the legitimacy of his offspring. "I am like you, they say," avers his son Mamillius; "Why, that's some comfort," replies doubtful Leontes (I.ii.208). His wife is pregnant again, though, and he's positive the child's a bastard. "'Tis Polixenes/ Has made thee swell thus," he accuses her, referring to his former best friend (II.i.61–62). And when the baby girl is born, he orders it killed:

> This brat is none of mine,
> It is the issue of Polixenes.
> Hence with it, and together with the dam [mother]
> Commit them to the fire!

II.iii.93–96

"It is a wise father that knows his own child," says Launcelot in *The Merchant of Venice,* mangling a proverb (II.ii.76–77). If that's true, then Leontes is a colossal fool.

The problem with illegitimacy is that it threatens a man's faith in what's truly "his"; it tortures him to think his estate might pass to someone else's progeny. Shakespeare's jealous men see their wives and children as property, and their property as extensions of themselves, so adultery is not only theft but also a kind of spiritual violation. "I had rather be a toad," Othello declares,

> And live upon the vapor of a dungeon
> Than keep a corner in the thing I love
> For others' uses.

Othello, III.iii.270–73

As in many other things, Leontes is of Othello's mind:

> There have been
> (Or I am much deceiv'd) cuckolds ere now,
> And many a man there is (even at this present,
> Now, while I speak this) holds his wife by th' arm,
> That little thinks she has been sluic'd in 's absence,
> And his pond fish'd by his next neighbor—by
> Sir Smile, his neighbor. Nay, there's comfort in't,
> Whiles other men have gates, and those gates open'd,
> As mine, against their will.

WT, I.ii.190–98

His wife Hermione is a pond, outrageously "sluic'd" and "fish'd" by treacherous neighbors, who break through Leontes' "gates." Slightly more mundane is Master Ford's metaphor, addressed to himself: "There's a hole made in your best coat, Master Ford. This 'tis to be married!" (*Wives,* III.v.141–42). "I'll be horn-mad," he later predicts (152).

■ ■ ■

In his misery, Leontes is happy for company; he consoles himself with the thought that other men are cuckolds too. The thinking seems to be: "She's not cheating on me because I'm inadequate, but because all women cheat." "Yet 'tis the plague of great ones," Othello muses; "...'Tis destiny unshunnable, like death" (*Othello,* III.iii.273–75). In the words of the song, "Your marriage comes by destiny,/ Your cuckoo sings by kind" (*AWW,* I.iii.62–63).

Of all Shakespeare's characters, Posthumus takes this idea the farthest, which is a real feat. He's so disgusted with women and their two-faced wiles that he rues, Hamlet-like, that there's no way for men to be born "but women/ Must be half-workers" (*Cymbeline,* II.v.1–2). And since they are,

> We are all bastards,
> And that most venerable man which I
> Did call my father, was I know not where
> When I was stamp'd. Some coiner with his tools*
> Made me a counterfeit; yet my mother seem'd
> The Dian of that time. So doth my wife
> The nonpareil of this.

> II.v.2–8

---

* See "tool," page 204.

"Dian" is the Latin goddess Diana (the Greek Artemis), whose fierce defense of her own virginity was legendary. Posthumus thought his mother a very Diana; his wife seemed even more pure—pure beyond compare ("nonpareil"); but now he "knows" it was all false seeming. After seething for a few more lines over Imogen's refusal to sleep with him before they were married, Posthumus turns his deranged thoughts to "yellow Iachimo," the smooth Italian he thinks conquered his wife in less than an hour: "Perchance he spoke not, but/ Like a full-acorn'd boar, a German one,/ Cried 'O!' and mounted" (15–17).

Convinced that all women are lying whores, Posthumus next delivers his notorious indictment of the sex:

> Could I find out
> The woman's part in me—for there's no motion
> That tends to vice in man, but I affirm
> It is the woman's part: be it lying, note it,
> The woman's; flattering, hers; deceiving, hers;
> Lust and rank thoughts, hers, hers; revenges, hers;
> Ambitions, covetings, change of prides [fashions],
>   disdain,
> Nice [wanton] longing, slanders, mutability,
> All faults that name, nay, that hell knows,
> Why, hers, in part or all; but rather, all;
> For even to vice
> They are not constant, but are changing still:
> One vice but of a minute old, for one
> Not half so old as that.

19–32

This is a truly impressive rant. And while the horn-mad Posthumus is indeed a fool, it's hard not to feel that Shakespeare had some feeling for what he was writing.

■ ■ ■

Few males in Shakespeare, however, are mad enough to believe that *every* wife is untrue; but this still leaves the worrisome question: Does the cuckoo sing for thee? Answering it turns out to be the problem. If your wife is true and you know it, that's best; if she's false and you don't, well then what you don't know won't hurt you. If she's false and you know it, that's bad, but at least you know; if you suspect but don't know, that's worst. At least that's Iago's theory:

> O, beware, my lord, of jealousy!
> It is the green-ey'd monster which doth mock
> The meat it feeds on. That cuckold lives in bliss
> Who, certain of his fate, loves not his wronger;
> But O, what damned minutes tells he o'er
> Who dotes, yet doubts; suspects, yet strongly loves!
>
> *Othello,* III.iii.165–70

This is a remarkable performance. Having created Othello's doubts, Iago now convincingly sells him the notion that it's better to believe your wife false than to only suspect it. Suspicion is torture, certainty relief. "Villain," Othello swears to Iago, "be sure thou prove my love a whore;/ Be sure of it" (III.iii.359–60). The Moor rapidly buys Iago's wares, and as his doubt turns to despair, he dutifully reads from Iago's script:

> What sense had I in her stol'n hours of lust?
> I saw't not, thought it not; it harm'd not me.
> I slept the next night well, fed well, was free and
>   merry;
> I found not Cassio's kisses on her lips.
> He that is robb'd, not wanting what is stol'n,
> Let him not know't, and he's not robb'd at all....
> I had been happy, if the general camp,

Pioners and all, had tasted her sweet body,
So I had nothing known.

Othello, III.iii.338–47

The Clown in *All's Well* looks at things very differently. He knows he's destined for cuckolding, but also knows he can't prevent it, so he makes the best of a bad situation. In fact, he plans to enjoy it:

The knaves come to do that for me which I am a-weary of. He that eats my land spares my team, and gives me leave to inn [harvest] the crop. If I be his cuckold, he's my drudge. He that comforts my wife is the cherisher of my flesh and blood; he that cherishes my flesh and blood loves my flesh and blood; he that loves my flesh and blood is my friend: *ergo,* he that kisses my wife is my friend.

AWW, I.iii.43–50

Needless to say, the wittol Clown's cavalier attitude isn't shared by most of Shakespeare's characters. Here are a few of the things they have to say:

■ ■ ■

In *As You Like It*, Touchstone (interesting name) upbraids the shepherd Corin for disgusting and immoral acts of animal husbandry:

That is another simple sin in you, to bring the ewes and the rams together, and to offer to get your living by the copulation of cattle; to be bawd to a bell-wether, and to betray a she-lamb of a twelve-month to a crooked-pated old cuckoldy ram, out of all reasonable match.

III.ii.78–83

All poor Corin is doing is breeding cattle and sheep, but
Touchstone pretends not to see a difference between animals
and people. Corin is like a "bawd" (pimp) who profits from
sex, unnaturally mating young ewes to decrepit "cuckoldy"
rams, whose many "wives" all sleep around.

■ ■ ■

Moonshine. This lanthorn doth the horned moon pre-
    sent—
Demetrius. He should have worn the horns on his head.
Theseus. He is no crescent, and his horns are invisible
    within the circumference.

A Midsummer Night's Dream, V.i.240–42

The inept mechanics put on a play featuring the personified
Moon, "horned" because crescent-shaped. The word "horn"
almost always inspires somebody to make a feeble pun.

■ ■ ■

That a woman conceiv'd me, I thank her; that she
brought me up, I likewise give her most humble thanks;
but that I will have a rechate winded in my forehead, or
hang my bugle in an invisible baldrick, all women shall
pardon me.

Much Ado, I.i.238–42

This is Benedick in the full flush of his misogyny and cyni-
cism. He's happy a woman bore and bred him, but he doesn't
trust any others. A "rechate" is a hunting call "winded"
(blown) on a horn, which Benedick is loath to have placed on
his forehead. "Bugle" of course means horn again, while a
"baldrick" is its belt, invisible as the horn it holds. He might

also be glancing at the penile sense of "horn," in which case the "invisible baldrick" is closer to the female beltline.

Continuing with this theme, Benedick repudiates Don Pedro's suggestion that one day he'll find himself married, for "In time the savage bull doth bear the yoke."

> *Benedick.* The savage bull may, but if ever the sensible Benedick bear it, pluck off the bull's horns, and set them in my forehead, and let me be vildly [vilely] painted, and in such great letters as they write "Here is a good horse to hire," let them signify under my sign, "Here you may see Benedick the married man."
> *Claudio.* If this should ever happen, thou wouldst be horn-mad.

I.i.262–70

After Antonio has scolded her for being "too curst" (shrewish), Beatrice makes this witty reply:

> *Beatrice.* Too curst is more than curst. I shall lessen God's sending that way, for it is said, "God sends a curst cow short horns"—but to a cow too curst he sends none.
> *Leonato.* So, by being too curst, God will send you no horns.
> *Beatrice.* Just, if he send me no husband, for the which blessing I am at him upon my knees every morning and evening.

II.i.21–29

This is an odd joke, given that it would be Beatrice herself who gave her husband those horns. Perhaps she means "Without a husband, I can take my pleasure as I please and never be accused of horning him"—but that's a little more involved than the case seems to warrant.

■ ■ ■

As *Love's Labor's Lost* limps to its crippled conclusion—with four men facing penance rather than marriage—Shakespeare sends us off with a song:

> When daisies pied, and violets blue,
>   And lady-smocks all silver-white,
> And cuckoo-buds of yellow hue
>   Do paint the meadows with delight,
> The cuckoo then on every tree
> Mocks married men; for thus sings he,
>   "Cuckoo;
> Cuckoo, cuckoo"—O word of fear,
> Unpleasing to a married ear!

V.ii.894–902

Besides the obvious "cuckoo" pun, the tune also features maidens who "bleach their summer smocks" (no longer white?), and a character of doubtful reputation called "greasy Joan."

■ ■ ■

In *As You Like It,* a lord sings this ditty:

> Take thou no scorn to wear the horn,
> I was a crest ere thou wast born;
> Thy father's father wore it,
> And thy father bore it,
> The horn, the horn, the lusty horn
> Is not a thing to laugh to scorn.

IV.ii.13–18

Earlier in the act, Rosalind also jests on the horn. Disguised as a boy, she "pretends" to be Rosalind in order to tutor her heartthrob Orlando in the art of wooing. When he's late to one of their sessions, she grumbles that she'd just as soon be "woo'd of a snail":

> *Orlando.* Of a snail?
> *Rosalind.* Ay, of a snail; for though he comes slowly, he carries his house on his head; a better jointure [estate] I think than you make a woman. Besides, he brings his destiny with him.
> *Orlando.* What's that?
> *Rosalind.* Why, horns! which such as you are fain to be beholding to your wives for. But he comes arm'd in his fortune, and prevents the slander of his wife.

> IV.i.53–62

That is, a snail already has his horns before he's married, which means he's not beholding to his wife for them, saving her the trouble and saving her from blame for them.

■ ■ ■

In his mad speech contra marriage, Hamlet advises Ophelia to "Get thee to a nunnery, farewell. Or if thou wilt needs marry, marry a fool, for wise men know well enough what monsters you make of them" (*Hamlet,* III.i.136–39). In *King John,* the bastard Falconbridge threatens the Duke of Austria thus:

> Sirrah, were I at home,
> At your den, sirrah, with your lioness,
> I would set an ox-head to your lion's hide,
> And make a monster of you.

> II.i.290–93

The point of the "ox-head" is that it's horned.

■ ■ ■

You'll recall Leontes' essay on Sir Smile, who fishes his neighbor's "pond." To take us out on Shakespeare's last horn-mad note, here's the rest of Leontes' rant:

> Should all despair
> That have revolted wives, the tenth of mankind
> Would hang themselves. Physic for't there's none.
> It is a bawdy planet, that will strike
> Where 'tis predominant; and 'tis pow'rful—think it—
> From east, west, north, and south. Be it concluded,
> No barricado for a belly. Know't,
> It will let in and out the enemy,
> With bag and baggage. Many thousand on 's
> Have the disease and feel't not.

Winter's Tale, I.ii.198–207

Female lust and treachery are like a "bawdy planet," inexorably inflicting its evil influences "wherever it is in the ascendant" (Arden). After this excursion into Renaissance astrology, Leontes returns to metaphors of property and possession. There is, he says, no barricade that will block a woman's "belly" (womb) from assault, since the belly's bearer will let in the enemy anyway, along with his "bag and baggage" (most certainly references to the male equipment).

Parental Advisory: Explicit Lyrics and Bawdy Banter

L ondon's theaters—like its bear-baiting pits, brothels, and leper colonies—were exiled to the ghettos, called "liberties" because they were outside city jurisdiction. While life in the liberties was free, it wasn't easy—especially for a theatrical company competing with so many other exciting diversions. A trip to the playhouse was not for the faint of heart, and neither were most plays, whose spicing of adult themes and piquant dialogue appealed to the daring and discriminating consumer.

Of course, the Bard was not so crassly commercial as to mix in smut just to make a shilling. He mixed in smut to make a shilling *and* to make the plays better. The essence of Shakespeare's art is not its *morality* but its *moralities*. He does not rest on any particular theme or viewpoint; he produces multiple perspectives, some high, some low, some romantic, some rude. His sympathetic and inclusive mind saw contemporary life from a variety of angles; some were lower. He brought together all kinds and classes of characters; some were coarser. In short, he wouldn't be Shakespeare if he weren't a bit dirty.

Suggestive language and sexual innuendoes aren't confined to a few "bad" plays one could conveniently avoid (or especially seek out). It's true that some are racier (*Othello* leaps to mind), and some more tame (such as *Caesar*). Yet the distribution of bawdry through his work is widespread, even if it's not uniform. The careful reader can hardly hope to avoid it.

Shakespeare rarely resorts to the crudest or most shocking "adult" language, and nothing sexual is ever explicitly depicted. He was not insensitive to proprieties, so far as they went in 1600; nor did he spurn the traditions and standards of literary drama. On the other hand, the Bard's slang, puns, and double entendres were a lot more obvious then than they are now. Most everyone in his audience got the point, while today his archaic terms for sexual functions are apt to be mistaken for strange but no doubt elevated Shakespearean notions.

Though pervasive and unmistakable, the Bard's naughty material was left quite alone by royal censors, who had other fish to fry. (See "Will's Naughty Theater," page 12.) Which is lucky for us, since otherwise this book would be several chapters shorter. It would require volumes to catalogue the whole extent of Shakespeare's indecency, so I must content myself here with a mere representative sample.

I leave finding more to enterprising readers, who need only study any decent (or should I say indecent) modern edition of Shakespeare's works. Editors these days will at least note that a passage is "equivocal" or "suggestive," though they may not spell out the meaning in precise detail. On the other hand, bawdry is occasionally in the eye of the beholder, so your edition may not cover all the possibilities.

In this chapter I step through samples from the plays and poems, including dialogue, verse, and song. I offer a helpful but by no means exhaustive guide to the context, ideas, and language. I occasionally use explicit terms, in English and not in Latin, so *caveat lector.* Later, in "Shakespeare's Lewd Lexicon" (page 181), I concentrate more on the exact terminology, though again without exhausting the Bard's prodigious output.

■ ▓ ■

Shakespeare's best-selling work in his lifetime was not *Hamlet,* or *Henry IV, Part 1,* or any of his other famous plays. Rather, it was the now fairly obscure *Venus and Adonis* (1592–93), a narrative poem in 1194 lines. Published sixteen times in forty-seven years, *Venus* was especially popular with students, gallants, and other romantic young men who thrilled to its racy verses. They seem to have especially enjoyed the following stanzas, which are often alluded to in other literature:

> "Fondling," [Venus] saith, "since I have hemm'd thee
> here
> Within the circuit of this ivory pale,
> I'll be a park, and thou shalt be my deer:
> Feed where thou wilt, on mountain, or in dale;
>   Graze on my lips, and if those hills be dry,
>   Stray lower, where the pleasant fountains lie.
>
> "Within this limit is relief enough,
> Sweet bottom grass and high delightful plain,
> Round rising hillocks, brakes obscure and rough,
> To shelter thee from tempest and from rain;
>   Then be my deer, since I am such a park,
>   No dog shall rouse thee, though a thousand
>   bark."

229–40

The love goddess Venus is very poetic, which might distract you from what she's actually suggesting. To the chilly Adonis, finally locked in her arms, she offers all the delights of her body. Only rather than make her point plainly, she likens herself to a park where Adonis is welcome to feed. The curvaceous deity has many mountains and valleys to roam, and a pair of "pleasant fountains" south of her neck.

In the middle of the park, Adonis will find "sweet bottom grass" on the verge of her belly's elevated plain, and around the back are the goddess's two rising hillocks, which will lead him back to the grassy parts ("brakes") again. Sounds very enticing, but Adonis would rather be out hunting boar, which is interesting all by itself.

■ ■ ■

The romantic hyperbole in *Romeo and Juliet* would be just too ridiculous if it weren't offset by more realistic attitudes. The antiromantic Mercutio supplies the latter, in the form of earthy jokes and carnal catalogues—for example:

> *Mercutio.* I conjure thee by Rosaline's bright eyes,
>> By her high forehead and her scarlet lip,
>> By her fine foot, straight leg, and quivering
>>> thigh,
>> And the demesnes that there adjacent lie,
>> That in thy likeness thou appear to us!

Romeo, II.i.17–21

The daring Mercutio doesn't fear to joke with sorcery and spirits. Hoping to "conjure up" Romeo, he ironically incants the potent attractions of Rosaline, Romeo's current heartthrob. His references to the "demesnes" (domains) adjacent to her "quivering thigh" may remind you of *Venus and Adonis*.

> *Benvolio.* And if he hear thee, thou wilt anger him.
> *Mercutio.* This cannot anger him; 'twould anger him
>> To raise a spirit in his mistress' circle,
>> Of some strange nature, letting it there stand
>> Till she had laid it and conjur'd it down.
>> That were some spite. My invocation
>> Is fair and honest; in his mistress' name
>> I conjure only but to raise him up.

22–29

Benvolio, ever the caution, only provokes Mercutio to further outrage. Continuing on the theme of conjuration, Mercutio imagines "raising" a spirit in Rosaline's "circle." Why would this make Romeo mad? Because it leads into one long dirty joke, in which the spirit that stands straight until Rosaline "lays it" and brings it down is someone else's erection. Yet rather than anger him, Mercutio expects his banter will "raise up" Romeo.

> *Benvolio.*   Come, he hath hid himself among these
> trees
>   To be consorted with the humorous night.
>   Blind is his love and best befits the dark.
> *Malvolio.*   If love be blind, love cannot hit the mark.
>   Now will he sit under a medlar tree,
>   And wish his mistress were that kind of fruit
>   As maids call medlars, when they laugh alone.
>   O, Romeo, that she were, O that she were
>   An open-arse, and thou a popperin pear!
>
> 30–38

After a quick pun on "hitting the mark [target]" (as the spirit homes in on the bullseye), Mercutio explores a new vulgarity. His punchline is the zinger "open-arse," allegedly the naughty name young maidens lend a suggestively-shaped fruit (a kind of medlar). We presume that the "popperin pear" is shaped to fit the open-arse; and furthermore we note that "popperin" just happens to sound like "pop her in."

■ ■ ■

Mercutio lends more of this wit a few scenes later, after Romeo has been raised up and engaged in their ironical banter.

> *Mercutio.* Why, is not this better now than groaning for love? Now art thou sociable, now art thou Romeo; now art thou what thou art, by art as well as by nature, for this drivelling love is like a great natural that runs lolling up and down to hide his bable in a hole.
>
> *Benvolio.* Stop there, stop there.
>
> *Mercutio.* Thou desirest me to stop in my tale against the hair.
>
> *Benvolio.* Thou wouldst else have made thy tale large.
>
> *Mercutio.* O, thou art deceiv'd; I would have made it short, for I was come to the whole depth of my tale, and meant indeed to occupy the argument no longer.
>
> *Romeo.* Here's goodly gear!
>
> *Romeo,* II.iv.88–101

This repartee would hardly make sense, let alone qualify as witty, without its many dirty jokes. Mercutio's been trying to cheer up his lovesick pal Romeo, who's "groaning" with desire for Juliet. (Hamlet will later use "groaning" to mean "sexual moaning"—*Hamlet,* III.ii.267.) "Drivelling love" (that is, drooling or dripping love) is like a "natural" (idiot) who runs about looking for a "hole" to insert his "bable" in. A bable is a court jester's stick, fitted with a carved head at one end, and in this context a transparent phallic symbol. The term "hole" requires no comment.

Benvolio gets the joke and weakly calls for a stop. But this only eggs Mercutio on: He can't stop now, with his "tale against the hair." The line's surface meaning is that he isn't inclined to stop ("against the hair" means "against my wishes"). But "hair" clearly follows from "hole"—that is, his *tale* is *against* the *hair* but not yet *in* the hole. "Tale" is a homonym of *tail,* which is slang for "penis," as proved in Benvolio's retort ("Thou wouldst else have made thy tale large," i.e., "Otherwise you'd have had an erection").

As for the rest of the excerpt, here's a brief glossary: "whole depth of my tale" = "with the entire length of my 'tale' in the (w)hole"; "occupy" = "have sex with" (see page 195); "gear" = another slang term for "penis."

■ ■ ■

Romeo and Juliet continues to delight us with double entendres:

Nurse. God ye good morrow, gentlemen.
Mercutio. God ye good den, fair gentlewoman.
Nurse. Is it good den?
Mercutio. 'Tis no less, I tell ye, for the bawdy hand of the
    dial is now upon the prick of noon.
Nurse. Out upon you, what a man are you?

II.iv.109–114

This scene gives scholar Eric Partridge endless delight in his seminal work, *Shakespeare's Bawdy.* Basically, he thinks it's full of dirt. Indeed, the words "bawdy" and "prick" suggest that the foul-mouthed Mercutio's at it again. (We're only a few lines beyond the "bable" business.) And the Nurse does take offense, though we don't know exactly how much she understands of exactly what Mercutio's saying.

At the very least, "prick of noon" is indecent. "Prick" denotes "mark on a dial," so to be upon the prick of noon the hand must point straight up. Which is why it's a "bawdy hand"—not actually a hand at all. Or perhaps Mercutio refers to the groping hand of some lustful person. Partridge endorses this notion, though he does beg the question by using this conclusion to prove that "dial" means "pudend" [*sic*]. If you buy his idea, then the bawdy-handed individual is female. It's just as likely, though, that Mercutio means the hot hand belongs to the one with the prick.

■ ■ ■

An old hare hoar,
And an old hare hoar,
Is very good meat in Lent;
But a hare that is hoar
Is too much for a score,
When it hoars ere it be spent.

Romeo, II.iv.134–39

Ostensibly, Mercutio is singing of spoiled rabbit meat, which would only look "good" during Lent (when any meat at all was forbidden). But the appearance a few lines earlier of terms such as "bawd" (pimp) and "stale" (prostitute) puts "hoar" (moldy) in another light. Essentially, the last three lines mean "Even when you're desperate, a whore who's already done too much business just isn't worth the money."

■ ■ ■

It's not just Mercutio; when any Shakespearean character bursts into song, the chances are good that naughtiness impends. Take even the seemingly innocent lines sung by a page in *As You Like It:*

It was a lover and his lass,
    With a hey, and a ho, and a hey nonino,
That o'er the green corn-field did pass,
    In spring time, the only pretty ring time,
When birds do sing, hey ding a ding, ding,
Sweet lovers love the spring.

Between the acres of the rye,
    With a hey, and a ho, and a hey nonino,
These pretty country folks would lie,
    In the spring time, etc.

V.iii.16–25

This plot is straightforward: A country youth and his lovely lass make off for the fields to "lie" in the rye. And they don't just stare at the clouds: *lie* is the most common Shakespearean verb for sex. Capulet makes a macabre joke of it:

O son, the night before thy wedding-day
Hath Death lain with thy wife. There she lies,
Flower as she was, deflowered by him.

Romeo, IV.v.35–37

The present song takes a rosier view: lying feels great, and you should do it while you're able. Life is "but a flower," that is, it withers with age; "therefore take the present time" (*AYL*, V.iii.28, 30).

▪ ▪ ▪

The previous song is incredibly wholesome compared to those of the rascally thief Autolycus in *The Winter's Tale*. Where the clichés of springtime love are integral to "It was a lover and his lass," Autolycus takes them and rudely twists them:

When daffadils begin to peer,
    With heigh, the doxy over the dale!
Why, then comes in the sweet o' the year,
    For the red blood reigns in the winter's pale

WT, IV.iii.1–4

The little daffodils are innocent enough, but "doxy" sort of spoils the effect, since it was underworld slang for "begging wench." And then by the end of the stanza we're hearing how red-hot and ready for action the singer is.

The white sheet bleaching on the hedge,
    With hey, the sweet birds, O how they sing!
Doth set my pugging tooth an edge,
    For a quart of ale is dish for a king.

5–8

"Pugging" means thieving; linens were favorite pickings. The sweet songbirds make Autolycus think of fencing sheets for beer money.

The lark, that tirra-lyra chaunts,
    With heigh, with heigh, the thrush and the jay!
Are summer songs for me and my aunts,
    While we lie tumbling in the hay.

9–12

By now, spring is getting on, more birds join the chorus, and the singer is rolling in the hay with his "aunts," or whores.

■ ■ ■

Iago. 'Zounds, sir, you are one of those that will not serve God, if the devil bid you. Because we come to do you service, and you think we are ruffians, you'll have your daughter cover'd with a Barbary horse, you'll have your nephews neigh to you; you'll have coursers for cousins, and gennets for germans.

Brabantio. What profane wretch art thou?

Iago. I am one, sir, that comes to tell you your daughter and the Moor are now making the beast with two backs.

Othello, I.i.108–17

Iago is a rather unhealthy person, as he proves in this exchange with Senator Brabantio. To achieve the twin goals of provoking Brabantio and disguising himself, he deliberately coarsens his speech. But in this disguise, he's most like himself—profane, dirty, obsessed with animal sex. His incendiary "'Zounds" sets the tone (see page 87), which he maintains in his discourse on Brabantio's daughter.

If you've forgotten the plot, the young lady (Desdemona) has just eloped with a Moor (Othello). Iago wants to be the first to tell Brabantio the news, which he puts in an interesting context—that of a stable. While you're yelling at me, says Iago, your daughter's being "cover'd" (laid) by a "Barbary" (African) horse. Iago drives his bestial point home by referring to the future offspring of this gross and unnatural coupling. (Coursers and gennets are also horses, and "germans" means "relatives.")

"Making the beast with two backs" is the most memorable line in this episode, and Iago clearly relishes it. The lovers unite in their heat into a single deformed beast, which seems to sum up Iago's view of the process.

■ ■ ■

If you thought Shakespeare was above scatology, you were mistaken.

Panthino. Tut, man, I mean thou'lt lose the flood, and in
losing the flood, lose thy voyage, and in losing thy
voyage, lose thy master, and in losing thy master,
lose thy service, and in losing thy service—Why
dost thou stop my mouth?

Launce. For fear thou shouldst lose thy tongue.

Panthino. Where should I lose my tongue?

Launce. In thy tale.

Panthino. In thy tail!

The Two Gentlemen of Verona, II.iii.41–49

Panthino, urging Launce to board ship before the tide goes
out, launches into a potentially endless rhetorical train, when
Launce "stops his mouth" (apparently by clapping his hand
over it, though the expression usually refers to kissing). This
leads to the dirty business about losing one's tongue in one's
"tail" or backside—compare the modern variant, "he's got his
head up his ass." Both Launce and Panthino are quite familiar
with the old tale/tail double entendre, which we meet several
more times in Shakespeare (see page 203).

■   ■   ■

Sir John Falstaff may be old, fat, and diseased, but that doesn't
mean the ladies are safe—and neither is anyone else.

Hostess. Alas the day, take heed of him! He stabb'd me in
mine own house, most beastly, in good faith. 'A
cares not what mischief he does, if his weapon be
out. He will foin like any devil, he will spare neither
man, woman, nor child.

Fang. If I can close with him, I care not for his thrust.

Hostess. No, nor I neither, I'll be at your elbow.

Fang. And I but fist him once, and 'a come but within
my vice—
Hostess. I am undone by his going, I warrant you, he's an
infinite thing upon my score.

2 Henry IV, II.i.13–24

One of Shakespeare's dimmer characters, Hostess Quickly
spouts the filthiest talk without even realizing it. With each
word she utters, she gets herself deeper into double entendres,
no doubt emphasized with the lewd gestures by the actor.

We've never seen Falstaff come close to actually using his
weapon, but we've heard lots about his lascivious ways. So
Quickly's claim that he "stabb'd me in mine own house" is
more likely to suggest sexual aggression than the thrust of a
knife. "Most beastly" bears this notion along (think of Iago's
"beast with two backs"), and it all seems incredibly obvious
when you reach "if his weapon be out." In this context "foin"
(thrust) is particularly dirty, especially when we're told he does
it like the devil with anything that moves. (See "A Note on
Unnatural Acts," below.)

Fang, an equally dull-witted sergeant, plays along equally
unwittingly. "Close," "thrust," "fist" (meaning "grip"), and
"vice" (ditto) all conjure up grotesque couplings with the cor-
pulent knight. Quickly then concludes with a string of equivocal terms: "undone" (which often means "sexually violated"),
"going" ("go to it" means "copulate"), and "infinite thing"
(which I'll leave to your imagination).

▪ ▪ ▪

As he enters the Boar's Head Tavern three scenes later, Falstaff
sets off a virtual explosion of scurrilous jests and just awful language. His opening words are "Empty the jordan" (i.e., cham-

ber pot), which tells us where he's just been, and sets an appropriate tone for the subsequent discourse.

Next Falstaff engages in sweet banter with the prostitute, Doll Tearsheet. She is sick; he doesn't care; she wishes him "the pox" (VD); he jests that women like her "make the diseases" (II.iv.45). Falstaff then segues into the topic of "serving bravely," which is merely an excuse to make a series of sexual puns (see PIKE in "Shakespeare's Lewd Lexicon," page 196).

Things really pick up later in the scene, upon the arrival of the "swaggering rascal" Pistol, whose very name is a phallic pun.

> *Pistol.* God save you, Sir John!
> *Falstaff.* Welcome, Ancient [Ensign] Pistol. Here, Pistol,
> I charge you with a cup of sack, do you discharge
> upon mine hostess.
> *Pistol.* I will discharge upon her, Sir John, with two bullets.
> *Falstaff.* She is pistol-proof, sir; you shall not hardly
> offend her.
>
> *2 Henry IV,* II.iv.110–17

The literal meaning of "discharge upon" is probably "toast," but nobody really cares since the obvious secondary meaning is so much more interesting. It involves Pistol's discharging (firing) his PISTOL (page 197) on Quickly, which he promises to do "with two bullets." This threat is tricky, as "bullet" seems to take on several different lewd meanings as the scene progresses. ("Pistol-proof" is also confusing, but it seems to mean "unimpregnable.")

> *Hostess.* Come, I'll drink no proofs, nor no bullets. I'll
> drink no more than will do me good, for no man's
> pleasure, I.
> *Pistol.* Then to you, Mistress Dorothy, I will charge you.

> *Doll.* Charge me? I scorn you, scurvy companion. What,
> you poor, base, rascally, cheating, lack-linen mate!
> Away, you mouldy rogue, away! I am meat for your
> master.

> 118–26

Pistol's "master" is Falstaff, who seems to have some claim to Doll's "meat." Nonetheless, Pistol makes a move on her, she recoils and insults him, and then he rips her huge "ruff" (ruffled collar), which is part of her professional costume. When the Hostess objects, "not here, sweet captain," Doll is enraged that Pistol should be so honored:

> You a captain! you slave, for what? for tearing a poor
> whore's ruff in a bawdy-house? He a captain! hang him,
> rogue! he lives upon mouldy stew'd prunes and dried
> cakes. A captain! God's light, these villains will make
> the word as odious as the word "occupy," which was an
> excellent good word before it was ill sorted; therefore
> captains had need look to't.

> 144–150

Here is confirmed the fact that Falstaff's favorite Eastcheap tavern doubles as an informal brothel ("bawdy-house"). Pistol's diet is also suggestive, since "stewed prunes" were proverbially favored by prostitutes, themselves sometimes likened to prunes. (And "stew" was slang for "whorehouse.") To call Pistol a "captain" is to ruin a perfectly good word by bad association, as the word "occupy" has been ruined by its use to mean "insert one's pistol." (Compare Mercutio's use of the word, page 153.)

■ ■ ■

On the subject of shooting weapons, the merry French ladies of *Love's Labor's Lost* get bawdy with bows and arrows, as they jest with their companion Boyet. Shooting arrows first suggests the topic of deer hunting, which inevitably leads to jokes on "horns," i.e., cuckoldry (see "Horny Shakespeare," page 134). Rosaline parries with Boyet on this endlessly fascinating subject, leading Maria to proclaim that Rosaline "strikes at the brow." "But she herself is hit lower," Boyet giggles, alluding to the copulative connotations of "hit it." Then the pair of them burst into song:

> *Rosaline.* [*Sings.*] Thou canst not hit it, hit it, hit it,
>   Thou canst not hit it, my good man.
> *Boyet.* [*Sings.*] And I cannot, cannot, cannot,
>   And I cannot, another can.
>   [*Exeunt Rosaline and Katherine.*]
>
>   *LLL*, IV.i.125–28

The point of this scandalous tune is that while a woman may say no to you, she isn't therefore virtuous.

> *Costard.* By my troth, most pleasant. How both did fit it!
> *Maria.* A mark marvelous well shot, for they both did hit it.
> *Boyet.* A mark! O, mark but that mark! a mark, says my lady!
>   Let the mark have a prick in't, to mete [take aim] at, if it may be.
>
>   129–32

"Mark" means "target," but that's certainly less than Boyet has in mind. He's thinking of the female target of the male arrow, which is glanced at in "prick" (literally, the bullseye).

Maria. Wide a' the bow-hand [to the left]! I' faith, your
      hand is out.
Costard. Indeed 'a must shoot nearer, or he'll ne'er hit
      the clout [cloth, i.e., bullseye].
Boyet. And if my hand be out, then belike your hand is
      in.
Costard. Then she will get the upshoot by cleaving the
      pin.

133–36

The dialogue has now thoroughly degenerated. Maria's "your
hand is out" means much more than "your aim is off," and so
of course does Boyet's "your hand is in." Costard welcomes the
thought, looking forward to shooting off ("pin" is phallic, and
"cleave" here means "grasp"). "Come, come," Maria belatedly
protests, "you talk too greasily, your lips grow foul" (137). But
there's even more:

Costard. She's too hard for you at pricks, sir, challenge
      her to bowl.
Boyet. I fear too much rubbing.

138–39

Letting the obvious pass, I will just note that in lawn bowling
jargon, a "rub" is an obstacle (and thus Hamlet's famous
"there's the rub"); so "rubbing" in this sense means "hitting
obstacles."

■ ■ ■

Love, love, nothing but love, still love, still more!
    For O, love's bow
    Shoots buck and doe.
    The shaft confounds

Not that it wounds,
But tickles still the sore.
These lovers cry, O ho, they die!
     Yet that which seems the wound to kill,
Doth turn O ho! to ha, ha, he!
     So dying love lives still.
O ho! a while, but ha, ha, ha!
O ho! groans out for ha, ha, ha!—hey ho!

Troilus and Cressida, III.i.115–126

This extremely rude song, which simulates an orgasm, must have brought the house down. It also befits its singer, the old lecher Pandarus, who's been trying for two whole acts to steer Cressida (his niece) into Troilus's bed. Once again bows and arrows figure in an extended sexual metaphor, involving a "shaft" that "tickles" the "wound" it makes. After enough tickling the lovers cry out and "die," a word equivalent here to our word "come." Their sighs ("O ho!") and screams of "death" soon turn to laughter ("ha, ha, he!").

▪ ▪ ▪

The Welsh clergyman and schoolmaster Sir Hugh Evans has trouble pronouncing his v's. This leads him into trouble, as he tutors young William in Latin:

Evans.	What is the focative case, William?
William.	O—*vocativo, O.*
Evans.	Remember, William, focative is *caret.*
Quickly.	And that's a good root.
Evans.	Oman, forbear.
Mrs. Page.	Peace!
Evans.	What is your genitive case plural, William?
William.	Genitive case?

Evans.	Ay.
William.	*Genitivo, horum, harum, horum.*
Quickly.	Vengeance of Jinny's case! Fie on her! never name her, child, if she be a whore.
Evans.	For shame, oman.
Quickly.	You do ill to teach the child such words. He teaches him to "hic" and to "hac," which they'll do fast enough of themselves, and to call "horum,"—fie upon you!

The Merry Wives of Windsor, IV.i.50–68

First, Evans's "vocative" comes out as "focative," the closest Shakespeare ever gets to the F-word. Mistress Quickly feebly takes "*caret*" (it is missing) for *carrot,* which right after the "focative" line has obvious phallic connotations.

The fun continues with the declension of "*hic*" (this), in the genitive plural "*horum, harum, horum.*" Quickly is totally outraged that a grown man should be teaching a boy about whores, Jinny or anyone else. As for "hic" and "hac," *Riverside* guesses they mean "hiccup" and "cough," as from excess drink. This is a rather desperate gloss; most scholars agree something more naughty is meant, though few agree on what it is.

■   ■   ■

As Mercutio is to *Romeo,* Margaret is to *Much Ado:* the deflater of romantic balloons. When the newly engaged heroine Hero confesses that her "heart is heavy," her attendant Margaret irreverently replies, "'Twill be heavier soon by the weight of a man" (*Much Ado,* III.iv.24–27). Hero objects to the obvious naughty connotation, but Margaret is mock-innocent: If you interpret my words as naughty, it's the fault not of my speech but of your own "bad thinking" (33). A likely excuse.

Margaret excels at coy jokes that just skirt the edge of what's proper for a woman of her station (better than a commoner, but lower than a lady). Another fine example follows soon after, when Beatrice arrives, feeling even worse than Hero—her secret lovesickness has given her a head cold. "These gloves the Count sent me," Hero chirps, "they are an excellent perfume." "I am stuff'd, cousin," Beatrice sniffles; "I cannot smell." Margaret: "A maid, and stuff'd! There's goodly catching of cold" (III.iv.62–66). By brilliantly adding "maid" to the equation, she implies "by a man" after "stuff'd," which leads to her conclusion that this is a pretty amazing "cold."

Margaret gives more occasion for bad thinking in a later parley with Benedick, who asks her nicely to go fetch Beatrice.

> *Margaret.* Will you then write me a sonnet in praise of my beauty?
> *Benedick.* In so high a style, Margaret, that no man living shall come over it, for in most comely truth thou deservest it.
> *Margaret.* To have no man come over me? Why, shall I always keep below stairs?

> V.ii.4–10

Benedick's "style" puns on "stile" (bar), so "come over" means "climb over." At least until Margaret gets to it; by repeating Benedick's phrase, she turns it into a double entendre, and turns "come" into a sexual verb. Otherwise, her punchline doesn't follow. To "keep below stairs" means "to live downstairs with the servants," so the men upstairs would *always* be "over" her. Assuming the servants are women—which in this play they are—what she really means is that only with them will she escape being "come over" by sexually aggressive males. (For more of this exchange, see PIKE, page 196.)

■ ■ ■

Sir Andrew. I'll ride home to-morrow, Sir Toby.

Sir Toby. Pourquoi, my dear knight?

Sir Andrew. What is *"pourquoi"*? Do, or not do? I would
    I had bestow'd that time in the tongues [languages]
    that I have in fencing, dancing, and bear-baiting. O
    had I but follow'd the arts!

Sir Toby. Then hadst thou had an excellent head of hair.

Sir Andrew. Why, would that have mended my hair?

Sir Toby. Past question, for thou seest it will not curl by
    nature.

Sir Andrew. But it becomes me well enough, does't not?

Sir Toby. Excellent, it hangs like flax on a distaff; and I
    hope to see a huswife take thee between her legs,
    and spin it off.

Twelfth Night, I.iii.88–104

The sophisticated Toby is too witty for the dolt Sir Andrew,
who poses as a gallant man of the world, schooled in trendy
sports but not in anything difficult or useful, such as French.
In any case, when Toby hears "tongues," he thinks "tongs"
(curling-tongs), which leads to an appraisal of Andrew's un-
curled hair. In the final two and a half lines, Toby brings the
whole exchange to a head. A "distaff" is a yard-long rod for
spinning flax by hand, as huswives (housewives) were wont to
do. But *huswife* was common slang for "hussy" or "whore."
Thus Toby could mean either that the huswife will give Andrew a disease to make his hair fall out (see page 110), or that
she will spin on his distaff until *it* comes off (or simply just
comes).

■ ■ ■

Ophelia is between a rock and a hard place in her brief courtship with Hamlet. Her father forbids her from entertaining his suits, while he in turn goes "mad" and begins treating her indecently. In their most famous encounter, Hamlet screams, "Get thee to a nunn'ry, why wouldst thou be a breeder of sinners?" (*Hamlet*, III.i.120–21). "Or if thou wilt needs marry," he concedes, "marry a fool, for wise men know well enough what monsters you make of them" (137–39, a reference to cuckoldry).

This shabby treatment plus Hamlet's subsequent murder of her father drives Ophelia truly mad. In the most pathetic scenes in the play, she wanders the court singing seemingly random tunes that are nevertheless pregnant with meaning. Here's the most ironic, and most naughty, example:

> To-morrow is Saint Valentine's day,
>   All in the morning betime,
> And I a maid at your window,
>   To be your Valentine.
>
> Then up he rose and donn'd his clo'es,
>   And dupp'd [opened] the chamber-door,
> Let in the maid, that out a maid
>   Never departed more
>
> By Gis, and by Saint Charity,
>   Alack, and fie for shame!
> Young men will do't if they come to't,
>   By Cock, they are to blame.
>
> Quoth she, "Before you tumbled me,
>   You promis'd me to wed."
> "So would I 'a' done, by yonder sun,
>   And thou hadst not come to my bed."

IV.v.48–66

The scenario is this: A hopeful young virgin ("maid") sets off on Valentine's day to visit her fiancé. He sees her at the window, throws open the door, then throws her on the bed and takes her maidenhead. (No surprise: Young men will "do it" whenever they get the chance.) Once she's despoiled, he casts her off, explaining that the only way he was ever going to marry her is if he *had* to to satisfy his urges.

Mad Ophelia sings this song a few scenes before heading off to that big nunnery in the sky, where she'll never ever have to "do't." She seems to have taken Hamlet's warnings very much to heart.

■ ■ ■

The cocksure Clown in *All's Well* proclaims that he has an "answer will serve all men" (II.ii.13–14). The Countess is rightly dubious:

> *Countess.* Will your answer serve fit to all questions?
> *Clown.* As fit as ten groats is for the hand of an attorney, as your French crown for your taffety punk, as Tib's rush for Tom's forefinger, as a pancake for Shrove Tuesday, a morris for May-day, as the nail to his hole, the cuckold to his horn, as a scolding quean to a wrangling knave, as the nun's lip to the friar's mouth, nay, as the pudding to his skin.
>
> II.ii.20–27

This clown is one of Shakespeare's greasiest, which befits this greasy and somewhat distasteful play. But he is also clever, and his reply to the Countess is a Renaissance world in miniature. His answer, he says, is as fit for all questions as any other fit he can name, such as the fit of a fee in a lawyer's hand, the traditional pancake to Shrove (Fat) Tuesday, the skin on a pudding (sausage), and a few other interesting things, including:

- a French gold coin ("crown") to an expensively dressed ("taffety") whore, who rewards the payer with another sort of French crown (see page III);

- a country wench's mock wedding ring (made of rushes) on the frolicsome finger of her lover;

- a nail to its hole, which in this context is decidedly equivocal;

- a horn to the cuckold's brow (see "Horny Shakespeare," page 134);

- a shrewish hussy to a cheating knave, as they deserve each other's infidelities; and

- the lips of a wanton nun to the mouth of a frisky friar (see "Saucy Priests and Nuns' Lips," page 71).

▪ ▪ ▪

Bertram notifies his sidekick Parolles (who calls him "sweet heart") that he's just been forced to marry Helena. But he's not giving up that quickly. "I'll to the Tuscan wars," Bertram vows, "and never bed her" (*All's Well*, II.iii.273). Parolles is very glad to hear it and seconds that emotion:

> To th' wars, my boy, to th' wars!
> He wears his honor in a box unseen,
> That hugs his kicky-wicky here at home,
> Spending his manly marrow in her arms,
> That should sustain the bound and high curvet [leap]
> Of Mars's fiery steed.

278–83

Parolles' talk is often questionable, and there are several marginal terms in this speech. In a discussion about bedding or not bedding wives, "box" is not entirely innocent; and this in turn renders "honor" dubious as well. The "manly marrow" Bertram will not waste on his wife is more than just "vim"; and an epithet like "kicky-wicky" (which Parolles invents) can't mean anything nice. Partridge thinks it may derive from the French *quelquechose*, "something" (see THING, page 203); but you'd think that as a Frenchman Parolles could pronounce it properly.

■ ■ ■

> The codpiece that will house
> Before the head has any,
> The head and he shall louse:
> So beggars marry many.
>
> *King Lear*, III.ii.27–30

The Fool's song begins with a dirty-witty paradox, in which "codpiece" means "penis" (see page 184) and "house" means "find a residence," presumably in a fitting female place. Thus the first two lines mean "The man who screws around before he's got a roof over his head." The result is "lousy" for two reasons: (1) He's forced to house himself in his lover's hovel, where he'll be infested with lice, and (2) he ends up having to marry a pregnant doxy.

■ ■ ■

By the end of act IV, Lear—powerless, homeless, and mad—is "king" only in make-believe. But he enjoys revisiting the role in his bitter fictions:

When I do stare, see how the subject quakes.
I pardon that man's life. What was thy cause?
Adultery?
Thou shalt not die. Die for adultery? No,
The wren goes to't, and the small gilded fly
Does lecher in my sight.

King Lear, IV.vi.108–13

Recall Ophelia's observation that men will "do't if they come to't" (page 169). So far, Lear's rant is in keeping with his new theory that a man is just a "poor, bare, fork'd animal" with clothes on (III.iv.107–8).

Let copulation thrive; for Gloucester's bastard son
Was kinder to his father than my daughters
Got 'tween the lawful sheets.
To't, luxury, pell-mell, for I lack soldiers.

IV.vi.114–17

His wicked daughters may have been "lawfully" begotten, but Lear is wrong if he thinks Gloucester's illegitimate son, Edmund, is any better. "To't, luxury, pell-mell" means "Lust, do your thing, and promiscuously," for Lear wants an army of bastards.

Behold yond simp'ring dame,
Whose face between her forks presages snow;
That minces virtue, and does shake the head
To hear of pleasure's name—
The fitchew nor the soiled horse goes to't
With a more riotous appetite.

118–23

Luxury may be ready to go to it, but the dame Lear imagines affects resistance. Her simpering face promises "snow" between her "forks" (legs), that is, an icy reception. But she only makes a show of virtue, of displeasure at pleasure; when it comes right down to the business, she will act more riotous than any animal. ("Fitchew"—literally "pole-cat"—was also a term for "prostitute.")

> Down from the waist they are Centaurs,
> Though women all above;
> But to the girdle do the gods inherit,
> Beneath is all the fiends': there's hell, there's darkness,
> There is the sulphurous pit, burning, scalding,
> Stench, consumption. Fie, fie, fie! pah, pah!

> 124–29

In the end, this coy dame is just another woman: human from the waist up, beast from the waist down. (Which in fact makes them centaurs all over, since those legendary monsters were men above and horses below.) Lear assesses the female sexual zone and judges it a "sulphurous pit" that stinks, burns, and consumes. ("Hell" was slang for the area described.) This is a very impressive display of misogynistic disgust—chalk up another triumph for the Bard.

■ ■ ■

Perhaps the most deviant material in all of Shakespeare consumes half a scene in *Henry V.* It's so strange that I really must quote it at length:

> *Dolphin.* I once writ a sonnet in [my horse's] praise and began thus: "Wonder of nature"—

Orleance. I have heard a sonnet begin so to one's mistress.

Dolphin. Then did they imitate that which I compos'd to my courser, for my horse is my mistress.

Orleance. Your mistress bears well.

Dolphin. Me well, which is the prescript praise and perfection of a good and particular mistress.

III.vii.39–47

There's no Falstaff and thus a lot less gross corruption in *Henry V* than in the *Henry IV* plays. But there are still some remarkably rude scenes. Here we have the French crown prince or "Dolphin" comparing his horse to a lover, and the noble Duke of Orleance (Orléans) making strangely bestial jokes. To "bear well" means "carry well," but there's a pun on *bear* as "give birth" and another on *bear* as "endure the weight of (a man)." Which leads us to:

Constable. Nay, for methought yesterday your mistress shrewdly shook your back.

Dolphin. So perhaps did yours.

Constable. Mine was not bridled.

Dolphin. O then belike she was old and gentle, and you rode like a kern of Ireland, your French hose off, and in your straight strossers.

Constable. You have good judgment in horsemanship.

48–55

If it's the Dolphin's horse we're talking about, then the shaking's in the saddle. But if it's his *human* mistress, then the Constable means strenuous horizontal activity. To ensure her submission, however, the mistress must first be "bridled." The

Dolphin then jokes that the Constable's mistress must be at a mellower age, easily ridden with his hose off.

> *Dolphin.* Be warn'd by me then: they that ride so, and ride not warily, fall into foul bogs. I had rather have my horse to my mistress.
> *Constable.* I had as live [lief] have my mistress a jade.

56–59

But if you ride with your hose off, you must beware "foul bogs," a dark trap for a pantless gentleman. The very thought makes the Dolphin shudder, and we wonder what to make of his stated preference for horses. The Constable takes all this in stride, observing in return that he rather likes "jades" himself, meaning both old nags and easy women.

> *Dolphin.* I tell thee, Constable, my mistress wears his own hair.
>
> *Constable.* I could make as true a boast as that, if I had a sow to my mistress.
>
> *Dolphin.* *"Le chien est retourné à son propre vomissement, et la truie lavée au bourbier."* Thou mak'st use of any thing.
>
> *Constable.* Yet I do not use my horse for my mistress, or any such proverb so little kin to the purpose.

60–68

Then there's the matter of the Dolphin's non sequitur on hair, which generally stumps the annotators. Even if it's dirty it makes no sense; Shakespeare appears to have begun free-associating. How else to account for the curious joke about mating with a sow, and then the Dolphin's biblical quotation about dogs returning to their own vomit? The ultimate point, though, is that there's no accounting for tastes: Some men like horses, some pigs.

A Note on Unnatural Acts

Friendship and love weren't as sharply distinguished in Shakespeare's day as they are now. So you will find romantic terms in surprising places, such as the *Sonnets,* where the Bard effuses over a "beauteous and lovely youth" (54.13)—the Young Man he famously compares to a summer's day (18.1–2). Shakespeare even goes so far as to call him the "master mistress of my passion" (20.2), which is a rather wanton statement. But, regrettably, this boy with a woman's face and heart is "prick'd out" with a man's "thing" (20.12–13).

Despite the florid poesy, Shakespeare really only toys with the youth; he's flattering him, not making a pass at him. Nonetheless, in our own post-Freudian times, the sexual overtones of these platonic sonnets have come to seem less innocent. Tempting as it is to psychoanalyze the Bard, we must take into account the Elizabethans' less squeamish attitude toward intense male bonding. So long as the bonding didn't cross the line into actual sexual activity, they were content to allow men to *talk* like lovers. (The activity, however, was considered immoral, unlawful, and deviant, and could be prosecuted in the ecclesiatical courts.)

Men, or at least males, talked like lovers all the time in Shakespeare's theater. Women were forbidden to act on the English stage until after 1660, when the Crown was restored and the theaters re-opened. Until then, female roles were played by boys and even young men—some as old as 20. Which means that Romeo's famously romantic poetry was actually addressed to a boy dressed up as a girl. And it explains Cleopatra's predicate when she predicts that she shall be caricatured on the stage, where "Some squeaking Cleopatra [shall] boy my greatness/ I' th' posture of a whore" (*Antony,* V.ii.220–21).

That boys played female parts was unremarkable at the time, though it did cause the Puritans fits. Elizabethans were quite capable of suspending disbelief, and they had to be: On a stage largely bare of props and scenery, extra weight was invested in language, gesture, and costume. A boy who dressed and talked like a girl functioned in everyone's mind as a girl. Shakespeare relies on this fact in his plots as well as in his staging: When a female character dresses as a boy, she fools everyone. Of course, it's really a boy dressed as a girl who dresses as a boy, so the gender confusion is doubled, assuming "confusion" is the word. Perhaps "imagination" is more accurate.

In the text of his plays, Shakespeare imagines a whole range of possibilities for same-sex affection, though his nuances sometimes escape modern readers. Many have wondered, for example, about the "love" between Antonio and Bassanio in *The Merchant of Venice;* but it is only the strong bond between an older relative and a younger. Antonio *is* hurt and jealous when Bassanio marries; but that doesn't mean he's *sexually* jealous.

It's true, though, that other scenarios are a bit more curious. There are, for example, the sexual mixups in *As You Like It* and *Twelfth Night.* In the former, Rosalind disguises herself as a youth, whereupon the silly shepherdess Phebe falls in love with her. In the latter, Viola disguises herself as a youth, whereupon the silly countess Olivia falls in love with her.

Duke Orsino also finds the "youth" attractive. Meanwhile, the sailor Antonio swears up and down his love for Viola's brother. Also interesting is *The Merry Wives of Windsor,* where two simpletons inadvertently marry two disguised boys.

But all this is within the bounds of "natural" emotional folly. A few other cases, however, call for more serious attention. Hostess Quickly obviously refers to unnatural acts when she says that Falstaff "will foin [thrust] like any devil, he will spare neither man, woman, nor child" (*2 Henry IV,* II.i.16–17). But she doesn't even realize she's equivocating lewdly, so we can't draw any conclusions about Falstaff's indiscriminate predilictions.

There's no way to avoid the obvious meaning, though, in two plays that deal with Greeks and Romans, whose sexual tolerance was notorious. Everyone in *Troilus and Cressida* knows that the dissolute warrior Achilles has a thing going on with Patroclus. Insulted by the latter, Thersites rebukes him, "Prithee be silent, boy, I profit not by thy talk. Thou art said to be Achilles' male varlet"—that is, "his masculine whore" (*Troilus,* V.i.14–17). And in *Coriolanus,* when the exiled hero makes a pact with Rome's enemies the Volscians, their commander, Aufidius, declares,

> Know thou first,
> I lov'd the maid I married; never man
> Sigh'd truer breath; but that I see thee here,
> Thou noble thing, more dances rapt my heart
> Than when I first my wedded mistress saw
> Bestride my threshold.

Coriolanus, IV.v.113–118

We can only imagine what Aufidius's passion would have led to, since before it gets much farther he kills Coriolanus. Talk about tough love.

Shakespeare's Lewd Lexicon

■

onnoisseurs of Shakespeare's double entendres and outright dirty talk are directed to Eric Partridge's *Shakespeare's Bawdy* and, if that's not enough, Frankie Rubinstein's supplemental *Dictionary of Shakespeare's Sexual Puns* (see "References," page 209). The list below, which partly draws on both sources, only samples the riches of Shakespeare's naughty connotation, but it should satisfy most readers.

Both Partridge and Rubinstein are too enthusiastic; in overcompensating for the usual timid glosses, they also go overboard. If I don't think Shakespeare *meant* a phrase to be dirty, I don't include it here. On the other hand, many undoubtedly naughty words and phrases are missing from this list—that is, just because I don't list a term, that doesn't mean it's innocent.

Cross-references to other items in the lexicon are set in SMALL CAPITALS.

act of darkness

Edgar, posing as a former sinner, says he "serv'd the lust of my mistress' heart and did the act of darkness with her." Elaborating, he explains that he was "one that slept in the contriving of lust, and wak'd to do it" (*Lear*, III.iv.86–90). If "darkness" refers to the time of the act as well as to its wickedness, he must have "wak'd" before dawn. See also DO THE DEED.

assail, assault

Verb and noun, respectively, for laying siege to a lady's chastity. "Front her, board her, woo her, assail her," Sir Toby urges (*TwN*, I.iii.56–57). Praising the chaste Imogen as "goddess-like," Pisanio notes that she resists "such assaults/ As would take in [conquer] some virtue" (*Cymbeline,* III.ii.8–9). Also used in the *Sonnets* with the sexes exchanged: "Beauteous thou art," the Bard writes his Young Man, "therefore to be assailed" (41.6).

bawd, bawdry, bawdy, bawdy-house, etc., etc.

All these words refer in one way or another to the sex act. A "bawd" is a pimp or procuress; "bawdry" is either dirty talk or the dirty behavior; "bawdy" means "lewd" or "lascivious"; a "bawdy-house" is a whorehouse; and so forth. Pompey in *Measure for Measure* is a "bawd," as is the character Bawd in *Pericles.* "Come, sweet Audrey," Touchstone rhymes to his fiancée, "We must be married, or we must live in bawdry" (*AYL,* III.iii.96–97). In a nostalgic mood, Falstaff asks Bardolph to sing him a "bawdy song" while he reminisces on his youth, when he "dic'd not above seven times—a week" and "went to a bawdy-house not above once in a quarter—of an hour" (*1 Henry IV,* III.iii.13–17)

bone-ache

Pain due to veneral disease; or, by extension, the disease itself. "The vengeance on the whole camp!" cries the bitter Thersites to his fellow Greeks, who are fighting a war for a wanton woman; "or rather, the Neapolitan bone-ache!" (*Troilus,* II.iii.17–19). (Naples was considered the home of syphilis.)

bum

Buttocks. "Troth," Escalus tells Pompey, "and your bum is the greatest thing about you, so that in the beastliest sense you are Pompey the Great" (*Measure,* II.i.217–19). Apparently describing undignified flattering "curtsies," Apemantus mocks the "Serving of becks [precious nodding] and jutting-out of bums" (*Timon,* I.ii.231).

cliff

"She will sing any man at first sight," says Ulysses of Cressida. "And any man may sing her," Troilus bitterly adds, "if he can take her cliff; she's noted" (*Troilus,* V.ii.9–11). "Cliff," a variation on "clef," is also slang for the female parts. However, in *The Comedy of Errors* (III.ii.126), it probably means "breast."

clyster-pipe

Enema tube. Hoping to convince Othello they're signs of hanky-panky, Iago carefully notes Cassio's courtesies (such as kissing his fingers) to Desdemona. "Yet again, your fingers to your lips? Would they were clyster-pipes for your sake!" (*Othello,* II.i.176–77).

cock

One can hardly miss the vulgarity of "Pistol's cock is up,/ And flashing fire will follow" (*Henry V,* II.i.52–53; also see PISTOL). Outside such double entendres, *cock* was also a substitute for the even more shocking word "God," as in

"By Cock" (*Hamlet,* IV.v.61) and "Cock's passion" (*Shrew,* IV.i.118).

codpiece

In poetics this is called "metonymy"—the container standing for the contained. In Shakespeare, "codpiece," which denotes a decorative bag worn by fashionable men over their privates, very often means the privates themselves. On Angelo's decree that Claudio shall be put to death for fornication, Lucio exclaims, "Why, what a ruthless thing is this in him, for the rebellion of a codpiece to take away the life of a man!" (*Measure,* III.ii.114–16).

Elsewhere, Berowne calls Cupid the "king of codpieces" (*LLL,* III.i.184); and Borachio recalls a depiction of Hercules, whose "codpiece seems as massy as his club" (*Much Ado,* III.iii.137–38). Sometimes the metonymy proceeds another step, from the body part to its owner. "Here's grace and a codpiece," quips the Fool—"that's a wise man and a fool" (*Lear,* III.ii.40–41).

count

See FOOT.

dart of love

"Believe not that the dribbling dart of love/ Can pierce a complete bosom" (*Measure,* I.iii.2–3). The Duke means that Cupid's arrow is powerless against a well-defended ("complete") heart. But arrows are also phallic symbols, and "dribbling" is rather suggestive.

die

Have an orgasm. As Benedick begins to display the signs of lovesickness, his friends tease him mercilessly. They say the woman who loves him must not really know him or his "ill conditions" (bad qualities); yet in spite of that, she "dies for him" and "shall be buried with her face upward" (*Much Ado*, III.ii.67–69). When he gets around to proposing to the lady in question, Benedick vows that "I will live in thy heart, die in thy lap, and be buried in thy eyes" (V.ii.102–3). Suffolk puns along similar lines when he tells his lover, the Queen, that "If I depart from thee, I cannot live,/ And in thy sight to die, what were it else/ But like a pleasant slumber in thy lap?" (*2 Henry VI*, III.ii.388–90). Thinking he may be captured and executed, the mad Lear grossly puns, "I will die bravely, like a smug bridegroom" (*Lear*, IV.vi.198).

dildo

See LEAP.

do

The general, all-purpose verb for "have sex" (see subsequent entries for more specific predicates). The elderly Lafew jokes that "for doing I am past," i.e., too old (*AWW*, II.iii.233). "Yonder man is carried to prison," Pompey observes; "Well; what has he done?" asks Mistress Overdone; "A woman," Pompey replies (*Measure*, I.ii.86–88). (The name "Mistress Overdone"—for a character who runs a bawdy-house—is a dirty joke unto itself.) Similarly, when Chiron accuses Aaron of "undoing" his mother by getting her with child, Aaron quips, "Villain, I have done your mother" (*Titus*, IV.ii.76). "Young men will do't if they come to't," sings mad Ophelia

(*Hamlet,* IV.v.60), though she hasn't learned this through experience (see page 169). Further examples abound.

do naught with

"Naught"—meaning something worthless or wicked—is the root of "naughty," and so this expression is somewhat redundant, given the implicit meaning of "DO." But the clever Duke of Gloucester (later Richard III) risks redundancy for the sake of a pun. When Brakenbury protests that "myself have nought [nothing] to do" with King Edward's lover Mistress Shore, Richard replies, "Naught to do with Mistress Shore? I tell thee, fellow,/ He that doth naught with her (excepting one)/ Were best to do it secretly alone" (*Richard III,* I.i.97–100). See also NAUGHTY.

do one's office

I.e., "do one's job in bed," from the notion of conjugal "office" or duty. "And may it be," Luciana queries, "that you have quite forgot/ A husband's office?" (*Errors,* III.ii.1–2). "I hate the Moor," Iago explains, "And it is thought abroad that 'twixt my sheets/ H'as done my office" (*Othello,* I.iii.386–88).

do the deed

More redundancy (since "deed" also means "the sex act"), but at least it's alliterative. (Lysimachus's "do the deeds of darkness" — *Pericles,* IV.vi.29 — does it one better.) Berowne, who hates the thought of horns, fears that the lady he's fallen for is "one that will do the deed/ Though Argus were her eunuch" (*LLL,* III.i.198–99). He refers to the mythical Greek guardsman with hundreds of eyes, whose job was to guard Princess Io (who had been turned into a cow) from lusty Zeus. (Argus failed.)

The same myth conjoins with the same phrase in the Induction to *The Taming of the Shrew.* The Lord promises to show pictures of Io "as she was a maid,/ And how she was beguiled and surpris'd,/ As lively [realistically] painted as the deed was done" (*Shrew,* Ind.ii.54–56). He might call this art, but we call it pornography.

drab

Strumpet. Among the horrors in *Macbeth*'s witches' brew is "Finger of birth-strangled babe/ Ditch-deliver'd by a drab" (*Macbeth,* IV.i.30–31). Pompey the pimp refers to his whores and johns as "drabs and knaves" (*Measure,* II.i.234–35). Shakespeare's Joan of Arc is so awful that even her father calls her a "cursed drab" (*1 Henry VI,* V.iv.32). Given more to speechifying than to action, Hamlet curses himself for his compulsion to "like a whore unpack my heart with words,/ And fall a-cursing like a very drab" (*Hamlet,* II.ii.585–86). "Drabbing," uttered by Polonius earlier in the play (II.i.26), means "wenching."

emballing

When the maiden Anne Bullen (Boleyn) protests in *Henry VIII* that she "would not be a queen/ For all the world," the worldly-wise Old Lady returns, "In faith, for little England / You'd venture an emballing" (II.iii.45–47). The bawdy half of this pun should be obvious—to be queen, Anne has to sleep with the (still married) King. This is a variation on the theme, "What would tempt you to commit adultery?" which recurs, for example, in an exchange between Emilia and Desdemona in (*Othello,* IV.iii). It's the "literal" half of the pun that's now obscure. "Emballing" in the strict sense means "investiture with the ball and orb, the symbol of sovereignty" (*Riverside*, which shies from glossing the phrase any further).

erection

"They mistook their erection," notes Mistress Quickly, meaning to say "directions." Falstaff responds, "So did I mine, to build upon a foolish woman's promise" (*Wives*, III.v.39–42).

fall backward

One day a little girl, daughter of Juliet's nurse, falls on her face and begins crying. The Nurse's "merry" husband takes up the child and says, "Yea, dost thou fall upon thy face?/ Thou wilt fall backward when thou hast more wit,/ Wilt thou not, Jule?" (*Romeo*, I.iii.41–43). This joke doesn't strike anyone else as particularly funny. It means: "When you're older, you'll fall on your back for men." The picture is a little clearer as the love goddess Venus wrestles Adonis into an amorous pose: "He on her belly falls, she on her back" (*Venus*, 594)—and thus "Her champion [is] mounted for the hot encounter" (596).

fig

Not just a fruit, but an expletive accompanied by an obscene gesture, similar to "giving the finger." In Italian, the gesture's native language, the word is *fico*, which like *fig* refers back to another F-word. Both versions are Ancient Pistol's trademarks, his indignant replies to perceived accusations. "'Steal'? foh! a *fico* for the phrase!" (*Wives*, I.iii.30); "When Pistol lies, do this [*makes gesture*], and fig me like/ The bragging Spaniard"

(*2 Henry IV*, V.iii.118–19). Iago contributes "Bless'd fig's-end!" in *Othello* (II.i.251).

finger

According to Thersites, "the devil Luxury" (lust) has a "fat rump" and "potato finger" (*Troilus*, V.ii.55–56). This sure sounds lewd, and almost certainly is lewd, but the point of the joke has been lost. The term "fingering" is more obviously bawdy in *Cymbeline*, when Cloten the clownish gallant hires musicians to help "penetrate" his resistant love object, Imogen. "Come on, tune. If you can penetrate her with your fingering, so; we'll try with tongue too" (II.iii.14–15).

foot, count

Frenchified versions of two ancient four-letter words, from *Henry V*: "Le *foot* et le *count*!" exclaims Kate. "O Seigneur Dieu! ils sont les mots de son mauvais, corruptible, gros, et impudique, et non pour les dames de honneur d'user" (III.iv.52–54). To translate: "The f—— and the c——! O Lord God! those words are bad, wicked, coarse, and immodest, and they should not be used by ladies of honor."

foutre

The word Katherine thinks sounds like FOOT. "A foutre for thine office!" Pistol hurls at Justice Shallow, whose authority has just expired along with King Henry IV (*2 Henry IV*, V.iii.114)

glass of virginity

When Marina refuses to cooperate with the bawds who
have captured her, Bawd (the madame) orders her assis-
tant to "take her [Marina] away, use her at thy pleasure.
Crack the glass of her virginity, and make the rest mal-
leable" (*Pericles*, IV.vi.141–43). The "glass of her virginity"
is her "VIRGIN-KNOT."

horn

The cuckold's invisible badge of shame, but also slang for
"erect penis." "Away, you three-inch fool!" cries Curtis.
"Am I but three inches?" retorts Grumio; "Why, thy horn
is a foot, and so long am I at the least" (*Shrew*, IV.i.26–28).
Benedick attempts to write a love poem, but he has trouble with the rhymes: "I can find out no rhyme to 'lady'
but 'baby,' an innocent rhyme; for 'scorn,' 'horn,' a hard
rhyme"—that is, as the baby is innocent, it's the *horn*
that's *hard* (*Much Ado*, V.ii.37–38). Perhaps also in *Venus
and Adonis:* "She hearkens for his hounds and for his
horn:/ Anon she hears them chant it lustily" (868–69).

huswife

"Housewife," but also common slang for "hussy, harlot."
(Brothels in Shakespeare's London were run out of sub-
urban garden houses near to the theaters.) Iago defines
the term by calling the courtesan Bianca a "huswife that
by selling her desires/ Buys herself bread and clothes"
(*Othello*, IV.i.94–95). This also illuminates his earlier un-
masking of wives as "Players in your huswifery, and
huswives in your beds" (*Othello*, II.i.112)—see page 132.
"Doth Fortune play the huswife with me now?" asks a
distressed Pistol (*Henry V*, V.i.80), meaning, "Does she

cheat me?" Cleopatra also refers to "the false huswife Fortune" (*Antony,* IV.xv.44).

jakes, jordan

Terms for a privy or outhouse. "Empty the jordan," Falstaff commands (*2 Henry IV,* II.iv.33). Costard jests on Alexander the Great's heraldic emblem, a seated lion holding a "poll-axe" (battle-axe): "Your lion, that holds his poll-axe sitting on a close-stool [chamber pot], will be given to Ajax"—pronounced "a-jakes" (*LLL,* V.ii.576–78).

jump

See LEAP.

lap

Crotch. Hotspur is unlikely to be innocent when, as music is about to begin, he calls to his wife, "Come, Kate, thou art perfect in lying down./ Come, quick, quick, that I may lay my head in thy lap" (*1 Henry IV,* III.i.226–27). Not only is "perfect in lying down" bawdy on its face—see LIE—but Kate recognizes the naughtiness, as she rebukes him: "Go, ye giddy goose" (228). See also the quotations from *Hamlet* under NOTHING, and from *Much Ado* (act V) under DIE.

leap

Arrogant Benedick had once declared that if ever he submitted to the yoke of marriage, his friends should pluck the horns from a savage bull and plant them on his brow. Late in act V, Benedick's on his way to the altar, and Claudio reminds him of his boast, promising however to gaily "tip thy horns with gold." Benedick sharply replies that "some such strange bull leapt your father's cow"—i.e., "screwed around with your mother" (*Much Ado,* V.iv.44, 49). Iago suspects the like of his own wife, in particular that "the lusty Moor/ Hath leap'd into my seat" (*Othello,* II.ii.295–96).

Synonymous verbs, such as *jump* and *vault,* at times have the same bawdy meaning. When a dull-witted servant describes Autolycus's songs of "dildos and fadings, 'jump her and thump her'" (*WT,* IV.iv.195), he proves his stupidity by judging them to be "without bawdry" (193–94). Dildo refers to either a natural or artificial male organ; "fading" is slang for "orgasm"; and "jump" and "thump" refer to how fading is produced.

lie, lie with, lie on

Equivalent to the modern *lay* (as in "get laid"). "The doctor lay with me," Portia confesses, while Nerissa reveals that "The doctor's clerk… last night did lie with me" (*Merchant,* V.i.259–61); they both intend everyone to interpret this sexually. Othello imagines the goings on between his wife and Cassio: "Lie with her? lie on her? We say lie on her, when they belie her [i.e., make her dishonest]. Lie with her! 'Zounds, that's fulsome!" (*Othello,* IV.i.35–37). "To tell thee plain," says King Edward to Lady Grey, "I aim to lie with thee." "To tell thee plain," the lady replies, "I had rather lie in prison" (*3 Henry VI,* III.ii.69–70). Cleopatra's clown reports on a "very honest woman—but something given to lie, as a woman should not do but in the way of honesty" (*Antony,* V.ii.251–53). And so on and so forth. See also Capulet's use of the term on page 156.

maidenhead

Literally "maidenhood" (female virginity); by association the hymen, or more generally the virginal female parts in their "hidden" or "unknown" state. "What I am, and what I would," says disguised Viola to haughty Olivia, "are as secret as maidenhead" (*TwN*, I.v.215–16). Jack Cade dreams that when he's king, "There shall not a maid be married, but she shall pay to me her maidenhead ere they [the newlyweds] have it" (*2 Henry VI*, IV.vii.121–23).

malady of France

Venereal disease; the "pox." "News have I that my Doll is dead i' th' spittle [hospital]/ Of a malady of France" (*Henry V*, V.i.81–82)—see POWDERING-TUB. Also see "Racist, Anti-Semite, Xenophobe" page 110.

male varlet

"Thou art said to be Achilles' male varlet," Thersites tells Patroclus. Patroclus: "Male varlet, you rogue! What's that?" Thersites: "Why, his masculine whore" (*Troilus*, V.i.15–17).

mount

Posthumus envisions Iachimo's conquest of his wife: "Perchance he spoke not, but/ Like a full-acorn'd boar, a German one,/ Cried 'O!' and mounted" (*Cymbeline*, II.v.15–17). Aaron the Moor plans to "mount aloft" his lover Tamora in *Titus Andronicus* (II.i.13). After Venus grabs Adonis by the neck and pulls him to the ground, her "champion" is "mounted for the hot encounter"; but

"He will not manage her, although he mount her" (*Venus*, 596–98).

naughty, naught

"Lewd" and "lewdness," respectively. The constable El-bow, whose sentences are not always logical, insists that Mistress Overdone's house is "a very ill house": "if it be not a bawd's house, it is pity of her life, for it is a naughty house" (*Measure*, II.i.76–77). "A paramour," says Flute, "is (God bless us!) a thing of naught" (*MND*, IV.ii.13–14). When Cressida bids Troilus back into her bedroom—for strictly honest purposes, of course—his expression is amused. "You smile and mock me," she notes, "as if I meant naughtily" (*Troilus*, IV.ii.37). See also DO NAUGHT WITH.

Netherlands

Literally "low lands," and also an anatomical location in *The Comedy of Errors*. Dromio of Syracuse describes a greasy wench he's encountered as "spherical, like a globe," and then goes on to "find out countries in her." "In what part of her body stands Ireland?" asks his master Antipholus. "Marry, sir," Dromio quips, "in her buttocks, I found it out by the bogs." After Dromio likewise locates Scotland, France, England, America, and the Indies, Antipholus inquires, "Where stood Belgia, the Netherlands?" "O, sir," Dromio sighs, "I did not look so low" (III.ii.114–39). Since buttocks are already covered, these must be the frontmost nether lands.

nose

Shakespeare was centuries ahead of Freud in noticing the phallic associations of this sense organ. In *Antony and*

Cleopatra, Iras and Charmian jest over the Soothsayer's prediction that both will share the same fortunes in love. "Am I not an inch of fortune better than she?" Iras jealously inquires. "Well," responds Charmian, "if you were but an inch of fortune better than I, where would you choose it?" "Not in my husband's nose," says Iras (I.ii.58–61). Doctor Freud might have called this remark an example of "displacement."

nothing

What women have between their legs. "Lady," Hamlet politely asks Ophelia, "shall I lie in your lap?" "No, my lord," Ophelia protests. "Do you think I meant country matters?" queries the naughty Prince, punning on a rude term for ladies' privates. "I think nothing, my lord," Ophelia uncomfortably avers. Hamlet: "That's a fair thought to lie between maids' legs." Ophelia: "What is, my lord?" Hamlet: "Nothing" (*Hamlet,* III.ii.112–21). This common euphemism lends new meaning to the title *Much Ado about Nothing.* See also THING, which may pertain to either sex. Shakespeare pulls off a double pun when he writes that his beloved Young Man was originally created female, until doting Nature added "one thing to my purpose nothing" (*Sonnets,* 20.12).

occupy

This word is *only* used bawdily in Shakespeare. Doll Tearsheet complains that it used to be a perfectly good word, until it "was ill sorted," that is, until it fell into bad company (*2 Henry IV,* II.iv.149). The full speech is on page 162, and the only other occurrence of the verb is quoted in Mercutio's speech on page 153.

pap

Nipple. Timon implores Alcibiades to lay total waste to Athens: "Let not the virgin's cheek/ Make soft thy trenchant sword; for those milk-paps,/ That through the window-bars bore at men's eyes/ Are not within the leaf of pity writ" (*Timon*, IV.iii.115–18). The virgin's bodice is apparently embroidered so that "window-bars" of fabric allow her nipples to show through. "Pap" refers to the male nipple elsewhere in Shakespeare.

pike

Strategically admitting himself defeated in a wit-war with Margaret, whose help he needs, Benedick says, "I give thee the bucklers"—that is, "I give up." (A "buckler" is a shield, symbolically given over to the victor.) "Give us the swords," replies fiesty Margaret; "we have bucklers of our own." (Swords are phallic symbols, so bucklers must also have been vaginal symbols.) Benedick: "If you use them, Margaret, you must put in the pikes with a vice [screw], and they are dangerous weapons for maids" (*Much Ado*, V.ii.17–22). The meaning of "pike" follows that of "sword."

Falstaff is coarser than the courtly punsters of *Much Ado*. As he defines it, to "serve bravely"—like a true soldier—"is to come halting off, you know; to come off the breach with his pike bent bravely, and to surgery bravely; to venture upon the charg'd chambers bravely—" (*2 Henry IV*, II.iv.48–52). Out of this medley of military terms, "pike" and "breach" connote the same things as "sword" and "buckler." The rest is left to the reader's imagination, especially the part about "surgery."

pillicock

After Lear likens his daughters to pelicans (thought to drink their mother's blood), Edgar bursts into song: "Pillicock sat on Pillicock-Hill, alow! alow, loo, loo!" (*Lear,* III.iv.76–77). He's paraphrasing an old rhyme with dirty overtones ("cocks" sitting on "hills," indeed). "Pillicock" is an obsolete vulgarity, deriving from the Norwegian slang "pill" (penis) and the Anglo-Saxon slang "COCK."

pistol

Given his explosive temperament and rapid-fire profanity, Ancient Pistol is aptly named indeed. Part of the joke is that *pistol* was also slang for PILLICOCK. For a lengthy riff on the name, see above.

pizzle

"The part in beasts official to the discharge of urine" (Schmidt). The joke of Hostess Quickly's calling Pistol "Captain Peesel" (*2 Henry IV,* II.iv.161) is that that's how *pizzle* was pronounced. In a fit of pique, Falstaff had earlier called Prince Hal "you starveling, you eel-skin, you dried neat's tongue, you bull's pizzle, you stock-fish!" (*1 Henry IV,* II.iv.244–45).

play

To sport wantonly. Discoursing on the infidelities of wives, Iago notes that they "rise to play, and go to bed to work" (*Othello,* II.i.115)—that is, they have fun in the daytime with their lovers, and act like it's a job at night with their husbands. When Cleopatra invites her waiting woman Charmian to play billiards, the latter complains of a sore arm and tells the queen to play with Mardian, a eunuch. "As well a woman with an eunuch play'd/ As with a woman," Cleopatra puns (*Antony,* II.v.5–6). Perdita imagines strewing flowers on a riverbank for "love to lie and play on" (*WT,* IV.iv.130—see also LIE).

plough

"Royal wench!" marvels Agrippa; "She [Cleopatra] made great Caesar lay his sword to bed;/ He ploughed her, and she cropp'd [gave birth]" (*Antony,* II.ii.227–29). "And if she [chaste Marina] were a thornier piece of ground than she is," the pimp Boult proposes, "she shall be plough'd" (*Pericles,* IV.vi.144–45).

potent regiment

Maecenas informs Octavia, Antony's wife, that "Each heart in Rome does love and pity you;/ Only th' adulterous Antony, most large/ In his abominations, turns you off,/ And gives his potent regiment to a trull," i.e., "whore," i.e., Cleopatra (*Antony,* III.vi.92–95). "Potent regiment" literally means "power of rule," but in this context it's deeply suspicious.

powdering-tub

A heated tub in which one was supposed to sweat off a venereal disease. "To the spittle [hospital] go," bids Pistol, in his usual baroque fashion, "and from the powd'ring-tub of infamy/ Fetch forth the lazar kite [diseased whore] of Cressid's kind,/ Doll Tearsheet she by name" (*Henry V,* II.i.74–77). The tub fails, for the next thing we know, Doll is dead (see HUSWIFE). "How doth my dear morsel, thy mistress?" Lucio inquires of the bawd Pompey; "Procures she still? Ha?" "Troth, sir," Pompey regretfully replies, "she hath eaten up all her beef

[worn out all her whores], and she is herself in the tub"
(*Measure,* III.ii.54–57). See also TUB-FAST.

pox

Venereal disease, usually syphilis. Falstaff's got it in
Henry IV, Part 2: "A pox of this gout! or a gout of this
pox! for the one or the other plays the rogue with my
great toe" (I.ii.243–45). "Now the pox on her green-sick-
ness [moodiness] for me!" cries Pander upon Marina;
"Faith," notes Bawd, "there's no way to be rid on't but by
the way to the pox"—that is, except by getting her laid
(*Pericles,* IV.vi.13–16). "A pox on" is a popular curse, applied to whatever the curser happens to find objectionable; "A pox o' your throat, you bawling, blasphemous,
incharitable dog!" (*Tempest,* I.i.40–41).

prick

An old slang term that generates numerous Shakespearean puns. "Let the mark have a prick in't," suggests
sly Boyet in *Love's Labor's Lost* (IV.i.132). The use of
"prick" for "arrow" lends a new meaning to "mark" ("target"). Recall that in *Romeo and Juliet,* Mercutio jokes that
if Love is blind, "love cannot hit the mark" (II.i.33). Mercutio later delivers the classic, "the bawdy hand of the
dial is now upon the prick of noon" (*Romeo,* II.iv.112–13).
"He that sweetest rose will find," rhymes jesting Touchstone, "Must find love's prick and Rosalind" (*AYL,*
III.ii.111–12).

privates, secret parts

Genitalia. Rosencrantz and Guildenstern tell Hamlet
they are neither sad nor over-happy—"on Fortune's cap,"
says Guildenstern, "we are not the very button." "Nor

the soles of her shoe?" asks Hamlet; "Neither, my lord," Rosencrantz replies. "Then," the prince continues, "you live about her waist, or in the middle of her favors?" "Faith," jests Guildenstern, "her privates we." Hamlet: "In the secret parts of Fortune? O, most true, she is a strumpet [whore]" (*Hamlet*, II.ii.228–36).

punk

Low-class strumpet. An overdressed low-class strumpet is a "taffety punk" (*AWW*, II.ii.22). When Mariana paradoxically states that she is neither a maid, a widow, nor a wife, Lucio helpfully notes that "she may be a punk; for many of them are neither maid, widow, nor wife" (*Measure*, V.i.179–80).

quean

In its mild sense, "hussy"; in its strong sense, "whore." "Throw the quean in the channel," Falstaff rages, when he learns that Quickly wants him arrested (*2 Henry IV*, II.i.47). "As a scolding quean to a wrangling knave" (*AWW*, II.ii.25–26). "A witch, a quean, an old cozening quean" (*Wives*, IV.ii.172).

rump

Rear end. See FINGER.

slut

Touchstone, angling to get Audrey into bed, says he hopes she is not "honest" (chaste); for honesty added to beauty is like honey added to sugar. Audrey counters that she is not at all "fair" (beautiful), therefore she hopes she is honest. "Truly," Touchstone philosophizes, "and to cast away honesty upon a foul slut were to put good meat in an unclean dish." "I am not a slut," uncomprehending Audrey protests, "though I thank the gods I am foul." "Well, prais'd be the gods for thy foulness!" Touchstone concludes; "sluttishness may come hereafter" (*AYL,* III.iii.33–41).

When the concubines Phyrnia and Timandra beg Timon for gold, Timon bids them, "Hold up, you sluts,/ Your aprons mountant"—which means, "lift up your skirts to receive the gold; you're used to it" (*Timon,* IV.iii.135–36). "Our radiant queen hates sluts and sluttery," Pistol uncharacteristically avers, referring to Queen Elizabeth (*Wives,* V.v.46).

sport

In the Duke's absence, his deputy condemns Claudio to death for getting his fiancée pregnant. Lucio is indignant: "Would the Duke that is absent have done this? Ere he would have hang'd a man for the getting a hundred bastards, he would have paid for the nursing a thousand. He had some feeling of the sport; he knew the service; and that instructed him to mercy" (*Measure,* III.ii.116–20). Venus prompts Adonis to "Be bold to play, our sport is not in sight" (*Venus,* 124); that is, no one can see us, so no one will ever know. After Othello and Desdemona leave the stage to (finally) consummate their marriage, Iago quips, "He hath not yet made wanton the night with her; and she is sport for Jove" (*Othello,* II.iii.16–17).

stand, stand to

To be erect. "When it stands well with him, it stands well with her" (*TGV,* II.v.22–23). Women shall feel me, claims

Sampson, "while I am able to stand" (*Romeo*, I.i.28). "To raise a spirit in his mistress' circle,/… letting it there stand/ Till she had laid it and conjur'd it down" (*Romeo*, II.i.24–26; see page 151). "The danger is in standing to't [literally: standing ground]; that's the loss of men, though it be the getting of children" (*AWW*, III.ii.41–42).

The porter in *Macbeth* includes "stand to" in his long list of euphemisms for physical readiness. Drinking, he says, "provokes, and unprovokes" lechery: "it provokes the desire, but it takes away the performance…. It sets him on, and it takes him off; it persuades him, and disheartens him; makes him stand to, and not stand to" (*Macbeth*, II.iii.29–34).

stones

In *Merry Wives*, Dr. Caius promises to do violence to his enemy, the Welsh parson Hugh Evans: "By gar, I will cut all his two stones; by gar, he shall not have a stone to throw at his dog" (I.iv.111–13). "Oh wall," sighs Thisbe in an amateur play, "…My cherry lips have often kissed thy stones" (*MND*, V.i.190). The Wall is played by a (male) actor, so "stones" reverberates. "And jewels, two stones, two rich and precious stones,/ Stol'n by my daughter!…/ She hath the stones upon her," wails Shylock in *The Merchant of Venice* (II.viii.20–22). This quickly becomes a public joke (think "family jewels"). The Fool in *Timon of Athens*, discoursing on the whoremaster, says that he sometimes appears like a philosopher, but "with two stones moe than 's artificial one" (II.ii.111); the "artificial one" is the mythical "philosopher's stone," thought to turn lead into gold.

strumpet

Prostitute. As *Antony and Cleopatra* begins, Philo nastily jokes that Antony, one of the three rulers of the Roman Empire, has been "transform'd/ Into a strumpet's fool" (I.i.12–13). The "strumpet" is Cleopatra, who's already had famous affairs with Julius Caesar and Pompey the Great. In *The Winter's Tale,* the innocent Hermione is "Proclaim'd a strumpet" by her jealous husband (III.ii.102). Likewise, Othello curses Desdemona as an "impudent strumpet" and a "cunning whore of Venice" (*Othello,* IV.ii.81, 89).

tail, tale

Petruchio to Kate: "What, with my tongue in your tail?" (*Shrew,* II.i.218); the suggestion prompts her to strike him. "Tail" could mean practically any sexy body part— probably "vagina" in this case. Mercutio uses it for the male counterpart (see page 153), and so does the Clown in *Othello:* when a musician asks, "Whereby hangs a tale, sir?" the Clown replies, "Marry, sir, by many a wind instrument that I know" (that is, near the place where one emits wind; *Othello,* III.i.10–11). For other meanings of *tale,* see the dialogue between Launce and Panthino, above (pages 159), and also *The Tempest,* III.ii.11.

thing

Sex organ, either male or female. "She that's a maid now," says Lear's fool, "and laughs at my departure,/ Shall not be a maid long, unless things be cut shorter" (*Lear,* I.v.51–52). Viola, disguised as a youth, jokes that "A little thing would make me tell them how much I lack of a man" (*TwN,* III.iv.302–3). Shakespeare rues the Young Man's manhood as "one thing to my purpose nothing"

(*Sonnets,* 20.12). Considering that the milkmaid he loves may be too "liberal," Launce intends to keep her mouth and her purse tightly shut. But "of another thing she may [be liberal], and that cannot I help" (*TGV,* III.i.351–52). "I am no thing to thank God on, I would thou shouldst know it" protests Mistress Quickly; "I am an honest man's wife" (*1 Henry IV,* III.iii.118–19).

tool

The Porter is amazed at the gathering crowd at the palace gates: "have we some strange Indian with the great tool come to court, the women so besiege us?" (*Henry VIII,* V.iii.33–35). He doesn't mean a screwdriver. Imagining his mother slept around, and that therefore he's a bastard, Posthumus posits that "Some coiner with his tools/ Made me a counterfeit" (*Cymbeline,* II.v.5–6).

top

Othello wants to be "satisfied" on the question of his wife's adultery; Iago wonders, "How satisfied, my lord?/ Would you, the supervisor [spectator], grossly gape on?/ Behold her topp'd?" (*Othello,* III.iii.394–96). The word obviously sticks in Othello's tiny mind, for later he boldly asserts that "Cassio did top her" (V.ii.136). Alexander Pope and some other editors found the word "top" too much to take, and softened it to "TUP," which makes no sense in these cases, since rams aren't involved.

treasure

A woman's sexual zone—especially a virgin's—is sometimes poetically depicted as a hidden box or chest full of sensual riches. The evil Iachimo plots to make Posthumus believe that he has "pick'd the lock and ta'en/ The treasure of [Imogen's] honor" (*Cymbeline*, II.ii.41–42). Consider the "loss your honor may sustain," Polonius advises his daughter, before you "lose your heart, or your chaste treasure open" to Hamlet (*Hamlet*, I.iii.29–32). In the first case, "honor" means "virginity"; in the second, "(sexual) reputation" or "market value." The rudest example is in *Titus Andronicus*: "There speak, and strike, brave boys, and take your turns;/ There serve your lust, shadowed from heaven's eye,/ and revel in Lavinia's treasury" (II.i.129–31).

trull

Wanton woman; whore. This is the name the Duke of Burgundy gives Joan of Arc (*1 Henry VI*, II.ii.28), and it's not the worst thing she's called. The evil queen Tamora gloats as her sons drag Lavinia off to be raped: "let my spleenful sons this trull deflow'r" (*Titus*, II.iii.191). See also POTENT REGIMENT.

tub-fast

Abstinence from food and drink while undergoing treatment in a POWDERING-TUB. The misanthropist Timon urges the courtesan Timandra to "Be a whore still.... Give [men] diseases...season the slaves/ For tubs and baths, bring down rose-cheek'd youth/ To the tub-fast and the diet" (*Timon*, IV.iii.84–88).

tup

Iago to Desdemona's father, Brabantio: "Even now, now, very now, an old black ram/ Is tupping your white ewe" (*Othello*, I.i.88–89). Originally a noun meaning "ram," by the 1540s *tup* referred to the mating of sheep. Its application in animal husbandry apparently made the word more bearable than TOP.

turd

The embarrassing result of the way the Frenchman Dr. Caius pronounces "th." Caius: "If there be one or two, I shall make-a the turd." Evans: "In your teeth for shame!" (*Wives,* III.iii.236–37). Evans's reply—which makes the point clear—was cut from the Folio and is not printed in *Riverside.*

virgin-knot

The hymen. The protective Prospero, having consented to a match between his daughter and Ferdinand, warns the latter that "If thou dost break her virgin-knot" before the ceremony, thou art in for a heap of trouble (*Tempest,* IV.i.15–16). (Prospero also interestingly refers to Miranda as "my gift, and thine own acquisition/ Worthily purchas'd"; 13–14.) In Shakespeare, terms for virginity are often interchangeable with terms for its physical sign, the hymen. The Bawd in *Pericles* refers to both when she orders her deputy Boult to assess and certify "with warrant of her virginity" the maidenhood of their newly kidnapped merchandise, Marina. This "warrant" (proof) will make her a valuable prize at auction. "Such a maidenhead were no cheap thing, if men were as they have been" (*Pericles,* IV.ii.58–61).

weapon

The male organ in an aggressive state. "'A cares not what mischief he does, if his weapon be out" (*2 Henry IV,* II.i.14–16; see pages 159–60). "Draw thy tool," Gregory urges; "My naked weapon is out," Sampson replies

(*Romeo*, I.i.31, 33; see also STAND and TOOL). "I saw no man use you at his pleasure," Peter tells the Nurse; "if I had, my weapon should quickly have been out" (*Romeo*, II.iv.157–58). See also PIKE.

whore

Used roughly fifty times in Shakespeare, most frequently in *Troilus, Othello, Lear, Antony,* and *Timon.* This isn't even counting compounds such as WHORESON (see below), though it does count a few uses of *whore* as a verb ("This is the fruits of whoring," observes Iago on Cassio's fall—*Othello*, V.i.115). The word so horrified the Victorians that it was exterminated from the stage and from some printed editions (such as Bowdler's; see pages 18-19). Ironically, not even Desdemona's apt pun survived: "I cannot say 'whore.'/ It does abhor me now I speak the word" (*Othello*, IV.ii.161–62).

whoremaster

"Frequenter of brothels." Often found in adjectival form as "whoremasterly." Thersites gives a rousing performance in *Troilus and Cressida:* "I would fain see them meet, that that same young Troyan ass, that loves the whore there, might send that Greekish whoremasterly villain with the sleeve back to the dissembling luxurious drab, of a sleeveless arrant" (V.iv.5–9). See also DRAB.

whoreson

"Son of a whore," used as an adjective. "Thou whoreson ass" (*TGV,* II.v.47); "you whoreson peasant" (IV.iv.42); "You whoreson villain" (*Shrew,* IV.i.155); "Ah, whoreson caterpillars" (*1 Henry IV,* II.ii.84); "hang, you whoreson, insolent noisemaker" (*Tempest,* I.i.43–44); etc. The name "Abhorson" (*Measure*) is "abhor" plus "whoreson."

will

Sexual desire, sexual organs, and William Shakespeare himself in *Sonnets* 135 and 136, too long and intricate to quote here.

wind instrument

See TAIL.

yard

Formerly a very common euphemism for "penis," though used only once in that sense in Shakespeare, as Boyet and Dumain heckle Don Armado. Armado: "I do adore thy sweet Grace's slipper." Boyet: "Loves her by the foot." Dumain: "He may not by the yard" (*LLL,* V.ii.667–69).

References

Charles Boyce, *Shakespeare A to Z* (New York: Dell, 1990).

John Gross, *Shylock: A Legend and Its Legacy* (New York: Simon & Schuster, 1992).

Andrew Gurr, *Playgoing in Shakespeare's London* (Cambridge: Cambridge University Press, 1987).

Samuel Johnson, *Samuel Johnson on Shakespeare,* ed. W. K. Wimsatt Jr. (New York: Hill and Wang, 1960).

The Oxford English Dictionary, 2nd edition (Oxford: Oxford University Press, 1989).

Eric Partridge, *Shakespeare's Bawdy,* 3rd edition (London: Routledge, 1968).

Marvin Rosenberg, *The Masks of Othello* (Newark: University of Delaware Press, 1993).

Frankie Rubinstein, *A Dictionary of Shakespeare's Sexual Puns and Their Significance,* 2nd edition (New York: St. Martin's, 1995).

Alexander Schmidt, *Shakespeare Lexicon and Quotation Dictionary,* 3rd edition, 2 vols. (New York: Dover, 1971).

Samuel Schoenbaum, *William Shakespeare: A Compact Documentary Life,* revised edition (Oxford: Oxford University Press, 1987).

William Shakespeare, The Arden Shakespeare, second series, 38 vols. (London: Methuen, 1949–82).

————, *Mr. William Shakespeares Comedies, Histories, & Tragedies* [1623], facsimile, ed. Helge Kökeritz (New Haven: Yale University Press, 1954).

————, *The Riverside Shakespeare,* ed. G. Blakemore Evans et al. (Boston: Houghton Mifflin, 1974).

————, *Shakespeare's Sonnets,* ed. Stephen Booth (New Haven: Yale University Press, 1977).

Phillip Stubbes, *The Anatomie of Abuses* [1583], reprint, ed. Frederick J. Furnivall (London: N. Trüber, 1877–79).

Index

The titles of Shakespeare's works are given in short form, along with the abbreviations I use throughout this book. Character listings include the plays in which they appear. The remaining entries comprise historical persons, authors, books, important events, nationalities, and a few concepts. Some names have multiple entries; for example: *Henry VIII* (the play), Henry VIII, King (the character), and Henry VIII, King of England (the historical person). Supernumerary figures (such as "First Lord" and "Old Lady") are omitted.